GREAT SCOTS
A CONDENSED BIOGRAPHICAL DICTIONARY
OF 1450 NOTABLE SCOTS

The author has always been a firm believer that Scotland is a nation in its own right. Far too often Scots are regarded as funny little men in kilts playing bagpipes, and eating porridge for breakfast and haggis for dinner.

In this work, which has taken over forty years to collect and began as a hobby, details have been obtained from memorial statues and tablets all over Scotland; from quiz programmes and interviews on the radio and TV, and in the latter stages from the Reference Library in Stroud.

The serious compilation of the work was triggered off after he had seen a letter in a magazine from an American correspondent who had written: 'The Scots: Who are they? What have they done?'

Certain personalities entered may be considered by some as less than Great; yet included, they show the width of the field in which Scots are active and prove the author's assertation that the Scots are certainly no 'yesterday's men'.

GREAT SCOTS
A CONDENSED BIOGRAPHICAL DICTIONARY
OF 1450 NOTABLE SCOTS

Compiled by
J. GEDDES

ARTHUR H. STOCKWELL LTD.
Elms Court   Ilfracombe,
Devon.

© J. Geddes, 1974
First published in Great Britain, 1974

SBN 7223 0597-4
PRINTED IN GREAT BRITAIN BY
ARTHUR H. STOCKWELL LTD.
Elms Court   -   Ilfracombe
Devon

INTRODUCTION

The purpose of this work is to set out in a condensed form and in alphabetical order, noteworthy Scotsmen and women through the ages. And to show the powerful influence Scots have made and are still making, worldwide in every field of human endeavour.

The material has been gathered from many hundreds of literary and factual sources and represents over eleven years of research, with careful attention to accuracy. But a work of this nature must, at best, leave much to be desired. Any attempt to cover entirely the vast field of endeavour and achievement by Scots down the ages, must regretfully fall very short of completeness. It may however provide a source from which to begin detailed research and evaluation.

(Signed)

1973.

John Geddes B.E.M.
'Highlands'
48, Besbury Park,
Minchinhampton,
Glos.

To
Johnnie Thomson of Scarfskerry
a great friend
and one-time cycling companion.

ACKNOWLEDGMENTS:

To Mr Alan Morley, Librarian, Stroud Public Library,
for helpful advice.
Capt. George Sutherland of Mill of Mey, Caithness,
for material.
Mr David Thomson, of Scarfskerry, Caithness,
for material.
Mr William Connold, of Minchinhampton, Glos.
for material and other assistance.

SPECIAL NOTE

A

ABERCROMBIE, John (1780-1844) of Aberdeen. Philosopher and Physician. In 1830 he published a work on the intellectual application of logical methods in science. Recognized as the first consulting physician in Scotland.

ABERCROMBIE, Sir Patrick (1878-1957) Architect and town-planner. Author of the "Greater London Plan".

ABERCROMBY, Sir James, 1st. Baron (1776-1858) of Dunfermline. Judge Advocate General, Speaker in the House of Commons (1835-39).

ABERCROMBY, Sir John (1772-1817) of Clackmannanshire. Army General. Distinguished himself in Egypt and France. Captured Mauritius in 1809.

ABERCROMBY, Patrick (c.1656-1716) of Aberdeenshire. Antiquary and historical writer, best known for his 'Martial Achievements of the Scots Nation'.

ABERCROMBY, Sir Ralph (1734-1801) father of Sir John. General in command of the expedition against the French in the West Indies in 1795-96. He shares with Sir John Moore the credit for renewing the ancient discipline and military reputation of the British soldier.

ABERCROMBY, Sir Robert (1740-1827) of Tullybody. Army General. Served with distinction in North America and Canada.

ABERCROMBY, Robert James, born 1898 in Whitburn. General manager Bank of New South Wales (1962-64), Chairman Australian Banker's Assoc., Courtaulds (Aust) Ltd., and Associated Portland Cement (Aust).

ABERDEEN, (George Hamilton Gordon) 4th Earl of (1784-1860) of Edinburgh. Prime Minister of Britain (1852-55). Foreign Secretary under Wellington and Colonial Secretary under Peel.

ABERDEEN, (John Campbell Hamilton Gordon) 7th Earl of (1847-1934) Governor-General of Canada (1893-98) and sometime Lord Lieut. of Ireland.

ABERNETHY, James Smart, born 1907 in Fettercairn. Became Legal Adviser to the Commissioner of Lands and Protector of Labour, North Borneo (1937), Food Controller N. Borneo (1941), and Resident Magistrate Tanganyika (1949).

ADAM, Alexander (1741-1809) of Forres. Writer. Author of 'Roman Antiquities' (1791).

ADAM, Sir Fredrick (1781-1853) Scottish General at Waterloo (1815).

ADAM, James (1730-94) of Maryburgh. Architect, brother and partner of Robert.

ADAM, Jean (1710-65) of Greenock. Poetess, best known by her 'There's nae luck aboot the hoose'. Believed to have died in a poor-house.

ADAM, John (born in Maryburgh) Architect brother of Robert.

ADAM, Robert (1728-92) of Kirkcaldy. World famous architect. With his brother James designed also the furnishings, fittings and furniture to suit the houses they planned. From the 1750s to his death Robert erected or made alterations to at least 45 country mansions.

ADAM, William (1689-1748) of Maryburgh. Architect. Father of Robert, James and John aforementioned.

ADAMS, James W.L., born 1909, Educ. Arbroath and St Andrews. Professor of Education, Queen's Coll. Dundee 1955–. Education Officer (Scotland) B.B.C. (1939-47). R.A.F. Education Service (1942-45).

ADAMS, William G.S., born 1874 in Hamilton. Professor of Political Theory and Institutions, Oxford (1912-33). Sec. to the Prime

Minister (1916-19). Lecturer McGill Univ. Canada (1931) and visiting Professor Univ. of Toronto (1949) South Africa (1953 and 1957).

AIRLIE, (David L.G. Wolseley Ogilvy) 12th Earl of, born 1893. Representative Peer for Scotland (1922-63). A Lord in Waiting (1926-29). Director, Barclay's Bank (1947-63).

AITCHISON, James, born 1899, Educ. Glasgow. Professor of Dental Surgery. Examiner in Dental Surgery Univs. of Belfast, Edinburgh, Liverpool and Leeds. Radio Dentist to the B.B.C. Visiting Professor Melbourne Univ. Australia and Otago Univ. New Zealand.

AITKEN, John (1839-1919) of Falkirk. Physicist, known for his researches on atmospheric dust, dew, cyclones etc.

AITKEN, John Thomas, born 1913 in Glasgow. Became professor of Anatomy at Univ. Coll., London in 1965.

ALEXANDER, Sir James Edward (1803-85) Scottish General in the Crimea (1855-56) and Maori war (1860-62). He was responsible for the preservation of Cleopatra's Needle.

ALEXANDER, Robert L., born 1913, in Edinburgh? Rear-Admiral. Became Vice Naval Deputy to the Supreme Allied Commander Europe in 1962.

ALEXANDER, Sir William (1567-1640) of Menstrie Castle. Poet and Statesman. Sometime Lieutenant for the Plantations of New Scotland (Nova Scotia).

ALISON, Sir Archibald (1826-1907) of Edinburgh. Led the Highland Brigade at Tel-el-Kebir. Wrote a treatise on Army Organization (1869).

ALLAN, David (1744-96) of Alloa. Artist and historical painter. Sometime referred to as the 'Scottish Hogarth'.

ALLAN, Douglas Alexr., born 1896 in Fife. Director of the Royal Scottish Museum Edinburgh (1945-61). Representative, Museums Assoc. to Canada and U.S.A. (1960) and Central Africa (1961). Was Director, City of Liverpool Public Museums (1929-44).

ALLAN, Henry Samuel, born 1892 in Saltcoats. Became Capt. Commodore of the Peninsular & Orient Steam Navigation Co.

ALLAN, Janet Laurie, of Strathaven. Appointed Commissioner of the Salvation Army in 1951. Territorial Commander, Salvation Army,

Western India (1951-54) and of Southern India (1954-57).

ALLAN, John A. Briscoe, born 1911. Adviser to Foreign and Commonwealth Office on Prison Services, Ministry of Overseas Development 1964—. On loan to Kenya Govt.

ALLAN, Robert Alexander, born 1914 in Cardross. Chairman Conservative Control Board of Finance (1961-66). Governor Harrow School (1968). Director Financial and Provincial Co. and other Companies.

ALLAN, Sir William (1782-1850) of Edinburgh. Historical painter, appointed Limner to the Queen in Scotland in 1841.

ALLAN, William Nimmo, born 1896 in Callander. Appointed Consultant on Irrigation in Sudan in 1947.

ANDERSON, Adam (? died 1846) Professor of Natural Philosophy at St Andrews. Contributed original papers on the measurement of the height of mountains by the barometer.

ANDERSON, Arthur, born late 18th century in Lerwick, Shetland. Pioneer and benefactor, co-founder of the world's largest passenger fleet — the P & O Steam Navigation Shipping Company.

ANDERSON, Sir Colin, born 1904 of Scottish descent. Director of P & O Steam Nav. Co., and Chairman of many Companies (1960-69).

ANDERSON, Sir David, born 1895 in Glasgow. Engineer and Principal, Coll. of Technology, Birmingham (1930-46). Published numerous papers on technical education.

ANDERSON, David F., born 1904 in Strathaven. Professor of Obstetrics and Gynaecology, Univ. of Glasgow 1946—. Examiner to Central Midwives Board for Scotland. Freeman of the City of Glasgow.

ANDERSON, Sir Duncan, born 1901, Aberdeen. Civil Engineer, road, rail, bridge and tunnel construction. Controller Caribbean Region Colonial Development Corp. (1951-53). Chairman British Oxygen Co., and Director B.O.A.C.

ANDERSON, Francis S., born 1897, in Aberdeen. Chairman Bacon Market Council 1964—. Director, British Sugar Corp., Ltd., 1960—. Was Director of Fish Supplies, Ministry of Food (1943-45) Under-Sec. M.o.F. (1946-54) and Chairman, International Wheat Council (1949-59).

ANDERSON, Ian, born 1891 in Morayshire. Member of London Stock Exchange for 33 years. High Sheriff of Surrey (1942-48). Member of the Queen's Body Guard for Scotland. (The Royal Company of Archers).

ANDERSON, James (1739-1808) of Hermiston, Nr. Edinburgh. Writer on political economy and agriculture. Invented the 'Scotch Plough'.

ANDERSON, John (1726-96) of Rosneath, Nr. Dunfermline. Scientist. Author of 'Institutes of Physics' (1786). Invented the 'Balloon Post' and a gun which in 1791 he presented to the French National Convention.

ANDERSON, John (1805-56) of Galloway. Missionary and founder of the Free Church Mission Madras.

ANDERSON, John, born 1896 in Beith, Ayrshire. Retired as Chief Scientist, Admiralty Surface Weapons Establishment Portsmouth.

ANDERSON, Sir John, born 1908 in Montrose. Chairman, Board of Customs and Excise 1963–. Secretary, Dept., of Health for Scotland (1956-59), and Scottish Home Dept. (1959-63).

ANDERSON, Rev. John George (1866-1943) of Orkney. Became Archbishop of Moosonee and Metropolitan of Ontario in 1940.

ANDERSON, John Henry (1814-74) of Aberdeenshire. Magician, known as 'The Great Wizard of the North'. Performed in the Adelphi, London, where he caught a bullet fired from a gun.

ANDERSON, Moira. Singer and concert artist. Became popular as a singer with 'The White Heather Club' TV series. Her own BBC-TV series 'Moira Sings' was well received. She has done several Commonwealth tours.

ANDERSON, Rona, of Edinburgh. Actress. Appeared in the BBC series 'No Wreaths for the General' (1963); 'Dr Finlay's Casebook'; 'Dixon of Dock Green' etc. Her films include 'The Prime of Miss Jean Brodie' (1969).

ANDERSON, Thomas (1819-74) Organic chemist, remembered for his discovery of Pyridine.

ANDERSON, William, born 1889 in Kirkmaiden. Became professor of Philosophy at Auckland University College.

ANDERSON, William G. Macdonald, born 1905 in Dundee. Director-

General of Works, Air Ministry (1959-63).

ARBUTHNOT, John (1667-1735) of Kincardineshire. Physician and wit, friend of Pope and Swift. Appointed Physician to the Queen in 1705. Wrote 'History of John Bull' (1712) and 'The Art of Political Lying'.

ARBUTHNOTT (Robert Keith Arbuthnott) 15th Viscount of. Major-General, Chief of Staff, Scottish Command (1948-49). Commander 51st. Highland Division (1949-52).

ARMSTRONG, John (1709-79) of Liddesdale. Physician and poet. Appointed in 1746 to the London Soldier's Hospital, and in 1760 Physician to the forces in Germany.

ARMSTRONG, Sir William, born 1915 in Stirling. Official head of the home Civil Service since 1968.

ARCHER, William (1856-1924) of Perth. Journalist and dramatic critic. Was instrumental in introducing Ibsen to the English public.

ARGYLL, (George John Douglas Campbell) 8th Duke of (1823-1900) near Helensburgh. Statesman and author. Held the offices of Lord Privy Seal, Postmaster-general, and Indian Secretary. His writings include; 'The Eastern Question' (1879), 'The Reign of Law' (1866), 'Primeval Man' (1869), 'Philosophy of Belief' (1896), 'Organic Evolution Cross-examined' (1896).

ARNOTT, Neil (1788-1874) of Arbroath. Famous as a doctor and practical scientist. Prolific writer on natural science. Invented many useful appliances.

ARROL, Sir William (1839-1913) Construction Engineer. Built the Tay, Forth and London Tower bridges.

AYTON or AYTOUN, Sir Robert (1570-1638) of Fifeshire. Poet. Studied law in Paris and became Ambassador to the Emperor. Wrote poems in Latin, Greek and French. He is credited with the little poem 'Old Long Syne', which possibly suggested Burns's famous 'Auld Lang Syne'.

AYTOUN, William Edmonstone, (1813-65) of Edinburgh. Poet, humorist and writer to the Signet.

B

BAIKIE, William Balfour (1825-66) of Kirkwall. Explorer, Naturalist and Linguist. Opened the navigation of the Niger. Constructed roads and founded a city state.

BAILIE, Isabel, born in Hawick. Singer. The only British singer to appear with Toscanini on three occasions. Toured New Zealand, Malaya and South Africa.

BAILLIE, Joanna (1762-1851) of Bothwell. Poetess and playwright.

BAILLIE, Matthew (1761-1823) of Shotts. Physician and Anatomist. Wrote the first treatise in English on morbid anatomy (1793). He was the brother of Joanna above.

BAIN, Alexander (1810-77) of Watten, Caithness. Invented the chemical telegraph in 1843. He also invented an electric clock (1851) and a fire alarm system.

BAIN, Alexander (1818-1903) of Aberdeen. Psychologist and writer on mental philosophy.

BAIN, David (1855-1933) of Reay, Caithness. Carriage and Wagon Superintendent with the Midland Railway (1902-19). Controller of timber supplies, Ministry of Munitions (1916-18).

BAIN, Sir Fredrick (1889-1950) of Banffshire. Director, Royal Ins., Co.; Liverpool and Globe Ins. Co. Chairman Chemical Control Board Ministry of Supply (1941-44), Chemical Planning Commission Min. of Production (1942-44) and several other Chairmanships.

BAIRD, Sir David (1757-1829) of East Lothian. In 1805-06 he commanded an expedition which successfully wrested the Cape of Good Hope from the Dutch.

BAIRD, John Logie (1888-1946) of Helensburgh. Invented Television in 1925.

BALFOUR, Sir Andrew (1873-1931) of Edinburgh. Novelist and expert on tropical medicine and public health. Made several important discoveries in protozoology.

BALFOUR, Sir Isaac Bayley (1853-1922) of Edinburgh. Botanist. Sherardian professor of botany at Oxford 1884—. Elected Fellow of the Royal Society in 1884.

BALLANTINE, James (1808-77) of Edinburgh. Poet and painter, revived the art of glass painting.

BALLANTYNE, Archibald M., born 1908 in Glasgow. Appointed secretary to Royal Aeronautical Society in 1951.

BALLANTYNE, Robert Michael (1825-94) of Edinburgh. Popular writer of books for boys; 'The Coral Island', 'The World of Ice', 'The Dog Crusoe' etc.

BALLIOL, Sir John (? -d. 1269) of Barnard Castle, Galloway. Founder of Balliol College Oxford.

BANKS, Sir William (1842-1904) of Edinburgh. Surgeon and professor of anatomy at Univ. Coll. Liverpool. Served on the General Medical Council and on the Council of the Royal College of Surgeons, England.

BANNERMAN, John MacDonald, Baron (life peer), (1901-69) of Kildonan, Sutherlandshire. Farmer. Chairman of the Forestry Commission (1942-57) and of the Scottish Liberal Party (1956-65).

BANNERMAN, William Burney (1858-1924) of Perthshire. Major-General, Surgeon-General Madras (1911-18). Elected F.R.S.

BARBOUR, John (1316-95) from near Aberdeen. Poet, studied in Paris. Held office in the household of King Robert II.

BARCLAY, William, born 1907, in Wick. Professor of Divinity and Biblical criticism, Univ. of Glasgow since 1963. Lecturer and broadcaster.

BARCLAY-ALLARDICE, Capt. Robert (1779-1854) Scottish soldier and sportsman, walked 1000 miles in 1000 consecutive hours in 1809. He was the sponsor and trainer of Tom Cribb, the English prize-fighter who retired unbeaten.

BARNARD, Lady Anne (1750-1825) daughter of James Lindsay 5th Earl of Balcarras. Writer. Author of 'Auld Robin Gray'.

BARNETSON, James C., born 1907, educated in Edinburgh. Major-General. Appointed Deputy Director-General Army Medical Services in 1961.

BARNETSON, William D., born 1917 in Edinburgh. Chairman and Managing Director Minted Newspapers Ltd. 1966—, and Chairman of Reuters Ltd since 1968.

BARR, Archibald (1855-1931) from near Paisley. Engineer, who with William Stroud founded the firm of Barr & Stroud, scientific instrument makers and pioneers in Naval Range Finders.

BARR, Robert (1850-1912) of Glasgow. Novelist and journalist. Became a reporter on the 'Detroit Free Press' in 1881. He collaborated with Jerome K. Jerome in founding 'The Idler'.

BARRIE, Sir James Matthew (1860-1937) of Kirriemuir. Playwright, journalist and author of considerable merit.

BARTHOLOMEW, John George (1860-1920) of Edinburgh, Map engraver and publisher. Best known for his system of layer colouring of contours.

BARTON, Andrew (? -d. 1511) Scottish Naval commander who cleared the Scottish coast of pirates, and in 1506 sent James VI three barrels full of Flemish pirate's heads.

BASSENDYNE, Thomas (? -d. 1577) of Edinburgh. Bookseller who in 1756 reprinted the 2nd Geneva version of the New Testament.

BAXTER, James (1886-1964) of Ayrshire. Philosopher and economist. Financial Sec. to the Egyptian Govt. (1924-29); Financial Adviser to the Govt. of Siam (1932-35) and to the Govt. of Burma (1937-43). Financial and Economic Expert to the Egyptian Govt. (1943-46).

BAXTER, James H., born 1894 in Glasgow. Professor of Ecclesiastical History, Univ. of St Andrews 1922—. Secretary of British Acadamy Committee on the New Dictionary of Mediaeval Latin.

BAXTER, Stanley, born 1926 in Glasgow. Actor on stage and TV. Appeared in 'The Amorous Prawn', an ugly sister in 'Cinderella', 'What the Butler Saw', 'Phil the Fluter', 'The Stanley Baxter Show' etc.

BAXTER, William T., born 1906 in Edinburgh. Professor of Accounting, London School of Economics 1947—. Professor of Accounting Univ. of Cape Town 1937—.

BEALE, Geoffrey H., born 1913 in Edinburgh. Lecturer and reader in animal genetics in Edinburgh, London and New York.

BEATON, Douglas M., born 1901 in Ross-shire. Surgeon Rear Admiral (Retired). Was Medical Officer in charge R.N. Hosp. Plymouth and Command M.O. Plymouth (1957-60).

BEATSON, George Stewart (? -d. 1874) of Glasgow. Surgeon-General and Principal Medical Officer to the troops in India in 1863.

BEATTIE, Arthur, born 1914 in Aberdeen. Professor of Greek. Lecturer on the classics at Cambridge (1946-51).

BEATTIE, Colin P., born 1902. Educ. Edinburgh. Professor of Bacteriology, Univ. of Sheffield, and in the Royal Faculty of Medicine of Iraq. Director of Govt. Bacteriology Laboratory Baghdad (1937-46).

BEATTIE, George (1786-1823) of Kincardineshire. Poet and Humorist.

BEATTIE, James (1735-1803) of Laurencekirk. Poet and philosophical writer. Best remembered for 'The Minstrel' (1st book 1771 and 2nd book 1774). Became a friend of Johnson and the poet Gray.

BEATTIE, William, born 1903, Educ. Jedburgh and Edinburgh. Librarian, National Library of Scotland 1953—. Chairman Standing Conference of National and Universal Libraries 1964—.

BEILBY, Sir George Thomas (1850-1924) of Edinburgh. Industrial chemist. Improved the shale oil distillation and invented a manufacturing process for synthesizing alkaline cyanides. Elected F.R.S.

BELL, Alexander Graham (1847-1922) of Edinburgh. Invented the telephone in 1875-76.

BELL, Alexander Melville (1819-1905) of Edinburgh. Teacher of elocution. Practised a system of visible speech.

BELL, Andrew (1753-1832) of St Andrews. Clergyman and Philanthropist. While Superintendent of an orphanage school in Madras he introduced the system of 'monitor assistants' which was later universally adopted.

BELL, Sir Charles (1774-1842) of Edinburgh. Anatomist and surgeon. Discovered the function of sensory and motor nerves. Facial paralysis, known as Bell's palsy is named after him.

BELL, George Howard, born 1905 in Ayrshire? Dean of the Faculty of Medicine (1954-56 and 63). Lecturer in Physiology at Dundee, Glasgow and Bristol.

BELL, Harry, born 1899 in Aberdeen. Scholar. Sometime adviser with UNESCO delegation, Florence. Produced several papers and articles on literary, historical and educational subjects.

BELL, Henry (1767-1830) of Linlithgow. Pioneer of steam navigation with the 30 ton steamship 'Comet', launched in 1812.

BELL, John (1681-1780) of Stirlingshire. Traveller and Physician to Russian and Persian Embassies (1715-18) and to China through Siberia (1719-22).

BELL, Sir John (1782-1876) of Fifeshire. General who distinguished himself in the Peninsular war. From 1828 to 1841 he was Chief Secretary to the Governor of the Cape of Good Hope. Was Lieut-Governor of Guernsey (1848 54).

BELL, John E., born 1886 in Edinburgh. Vice-Consul at Paris (1911); Boston (1912); Belgian Congo (1913-14); Magellans Chilie (1915-19); Santa Domingo (1920); Consul at Galveston, U.S.A. (1920-23); Portland, Oregon (1923-29); Bahia, Brazil (1930-32); Basle (1932-34). Consul-General at Cologne (1934-39); Zurich (1939-42) and Strasburg (1945-46).

BELL, Rev. Patrick (1799-1869) of Arbroath. Invented the mechanical reaper in 1826.

BELL, Vicars, born 1904. Author, lecturer and broadcaster. 'Death Under the Stars' (1949), 'The Dode' and 'Death has Two Doors' (1950) and 'The Flying Cat' (1964) are only four of his many publications.

BENNETT, James Gordon (1795-1873) of Keith. Journalist. Issued the first number of the New York Herald in 1835.

BENNETT, James Gordon (1841-1918) son and successor of James above. In 1870 he sent Stanley to find Livingstone and with the Daily Telegraph, financed Livingstone's Congo journey (1874-78). He also promoted polar exploration, yachting, motoring and storm warnings.

BENNETT, John, born 1893 in Ratho. Major-General, Director of Medicine and Consulting Physician to the Army (1947-51).

BENNETT, John Hughes (1812-75) of Edinburgh. Discovered the medicinal value of cod-liver oil.

BENNETT, Roland A., born 1899, Educ. Stornoway and Edinburgh. Major-General, Consulting Physician to the Far East Land Forces (1946-49). Director of Medicine to the Army (1955-59) and Hon. Physician to the Queen (1955-59).

BEVERIDGE, William Henry, 1st Baron, born 1879 at Rangpur, India of Scottish descent. Economist, best remembered as the author of the report on Social Insurance and Allied Services (1942) known as 'The Beveridge Report'.

BILSLAND, (Alexander S. Bilsland) 1st Baron of Kinrara, born 1892 in Glasgow. Sometime Governor of the Bank of Scotland, and Director of the Burma Oil Co. Ltd. and other Companies.

BLACK, Adam (1784-1874) of Edinburgh. Publisher. Achieved fame through the purchase of the Encyclopaedia Britannica in 1872, after Constable's failure, and of Scott's novels from Cadell's representatives in 1851.

BLACK, Joseph (1728-99). Chemist. He showed that the causticity of lime and the alkalies is due to the absence of fixed air (carbon dioxide) present in limestone and the carbonates of the alkalies. His fame rests chiefly on the theory of 'Latent Heat' which he evolved.

BLACK, William (1841-98) of Glasgow. Novelist and journalist. War correspondent during the Austro-Prussian war.

BLACKIE, John Stuart (1809-95) of Glasgow. Eminent writer, poet and Philologist.

BLACKWELL, Alexander (1704-47) of Aberdeen. Adventurer, agriculturist and self-appointed physician. Was beheaded in 1747.

BLAIR, Robert (1699-1746) of Edinburgh. Divine and theological writer. Author of 'The Grave' (1743).

BLAIR, Robert (? - d. 1828) of Murchiston. Invented the 'Aplanatic' telescope.

BLAIR-KERR, William (Mr Justice Blair-Kerr) born 1911 in Dumblane. Puisne Judge Supreme Court, Hong Kong 1961—. Director of Weapons and Engineering, Air Ministry (1958-60). On British Defence Staff Washington (1960-63).

BLAIR-OLIPHANT, David N.K., born 1911 in Blairgowrie. Air Vice-Marshal R.A.F. Vice-President (Air) Ordnance Board 1963.

BLAKE, George, born 1893 in Greenock. Novelist and journalist. Became acting editor of John O'London's Weekly in 1924 and editor of the Strand Magazine in 1928. Among his latest novels, the best known are 'The Valiant Heart' (1940); 'The Westering Sun' (1946); 'The Five Arches' (1947) and 'The Voyage Home' (1952).

BLANE, Sir Gilbert (1749-1834) of Blanefield, Ayrshire. Physician. Sailed with Rodney to the West Indies in 1779. As head of the Navy Medical Board was instrumental in introducing the use of lemon juice on board ship to prevent scurvy.

BLYTH, Chay, born 1940, in Hawick. Made the first east/west solo circumnavigation of the world in a sailing vessel. Rowed the Atlantic in 1966 with John Ridgway.

BOECE or BOETHIUS, Hector (c. 1456-1536) probably born in Dundee. Was first Principal of Aberdeen University. Wrote 'History of Scotland to the Accession of James III'.

BOGLE, George (1746-81) from near Bothwell. British diplomat selected as Envoy to the Lama of Tibet in 1774. The first Briton to cross the Tsanpu in its upper range. Became a personal friend of the Lama.

BOGUE, David (1750-1825) of Coldingham, Berwickshire. Minister and one of the founders of the London Missionary Society. He was also a founder of the British and Foreign Bible Soc. and the Religious Trust Society.

BONAR, Horatius (1808-89) of Edinburgh. Minister and hymn writer. 'I heard the voice of Jesus say', and 'I lay my sins on Jesus', his best known hymns.

BONE, Sir David W., born 1874 in Glasgow. Novelist and seaman. Went to sea at the age of 15 and rose to be Commodore in the Anchor Line. His books, which were all about the sea, included 'The Brass-bounder' (1910); 'Broken Stowage' (1915); 'The Lookout Man' (1923); 'Capstan Bars' (1931); 'Merchantman Rearmed' (1949) and 'Landfall at Sunset' (1955) an autobiography.

BONE, Sir Muirhead (1876-1953) of Glasgow. Painter and etcher. Official artist on land and sea in both world wars.

BOOTHBY, Lord Robert J. Graham, 1st Baron Boothby of Buchan and Rattry Head, born 1900 in Edinburgh. Politician and commentator on public affairs. Was secretary to the Chancellor (Churchill); (1926-29). President Anglo-Israel Assoc., and the British Association of Manipulative Medicine, etc.

BOSTON, Thomas (1676-1732) of Duns. Theologian, remembered chiefly for his 'Fourfold State' (1720), long recognized as a standard exposition of Calvanistic theology.

BOSWELL, James (1740-95) of Edinburgh. Man of Letters and biographer of Dr Johnson.

BOYD, Sir John, born 1891 in Largs. Brigadier and authority on tropical diseases and bacterial viruses. Hon. Secretary Royal Society of Tropical Diseases.

BOYD, Lachlan M., born 1904 in South Uist. Secretary for African affairs (1951-55). Minister of Local Government, Uganda (1955-60).

BOYD, Thomas J.L. Stirling, born 1886 in Edinburgh. Barrister-at-Law, Chief Justice Sarawak (1930-39); Air Ministry (1939-43). Chairman Works and Traffic Committee Westminster C.C. (1952-55) and Westminster Health Society (1956-59).

BOYD-ORR, Sir John, 1st Baron, born 1880 in Ayrshire. Biologist and nutritional expert. Director-General World Food and Agricultural Organization (1945-48). Winner of the Nobel Prize for Peace (1949).

BOYNE, Henry B., born 1910 in Inverness. Political correspondent The Daily Telegraph 1956—.

BRADDOCK, Edward (1695-1755) of Perthshire. General of a command against the French in America in 1755.

BRAID, James (1870-1950) of Earlsferry. Golfer. Was Open champion in 1901, 05, 06, 08, and 1910. News of the World tournament winner 1903, 05, 07 and 1911.

BRAIDWOOD, James (1800-61). Superintendent of London Fire Brigade. Was killed in a fire.

BREBNER, Sir Alexander, born 1883 in Edinburgh. Under-Secretary at Bihar and Arissa (1919) & Government of India (1919-23). Consulting Engineer to India Govt. (1927-29), and Chief Engineer India (1931-38).

BRECHIN, Sir David (?-d.1321), Lord of Brechin, Angus. Warrior called 'The Flower of Chivalry'.

BREMNER, James (1784-1856) of Keiss, Caithness. Engineer, Ship-raiser, Designer and Constructor of harbours. Was mainly instrumental in re-floating the grounded 'Great Britain' in Dundrum Bay in 1847.

BREWSTER, Sir David (1781-1868) of Jedburgh. Philosopher of great scientific attainments. Invented the Kaleidoscope in 1816 and developed the Stereoscope. Made important discoveries on the polarization of light. Elected F.R.S.

BRIDGES, John G., born 1901 in Glasgow. Director-General of the British Travel and Holidays Association (1945-63).

BRIDIE, James, (pen name of O.H. Mavor), (1888-1951) of Glasgow. Dramatist, Author and Playwright. His first London play was 'The Anatomist' (1931). He was for a time professor of medicine at Anderson Coll. Glasgow.

BRISBANE, Sir Thomas M. (1773-1860) of Largs. General and Astronomer. Governor of New South Wales (1851-1860). Brisbane the capital of Queensland is named after him.

BRODIE, George (c. 1786-1867) of East Lothian. Historian, remembered for his 'History of the British Empire from the Accession of Charles I to the Restoration'.

BRODIE, William (1815-81) of Banff. Sculptor. One of his major works is a statue of Queen Victoria in Windsor Castle.

BROGAN, Denis W., born 1900 in Rutherglen. Historian. Professor of Political Science at Cambridge and a Fellow at Peterhouse 1939—. Intelligence Officer with the B.B.C. during the second world war. Published a number of books on American history etc.

BROTHERSTON, John H.F., born 1915 in Edinburgh. Lecturer in social and preventive medicine, Guy's Hosp. Medical School and London School of Hygiene and Tropical Medicine (1948-51). Physician to the Queen (1965-68).

BROUGHAM, Henry, 1st Baron Brougham and Vaux (1778-1868) of Edinburgh. Law reformer, orator, debater and writer on an incredible variety of subjects including Mathematical and Physical Science, Metaphysics, History, Theology and Romance. Became Lord Chancellor. The Brougham carriage was named after him.

BROWN, A.B., of Edinburgh. In 1870 patented a servo-motor for hydraulic steering of ships by steam, air or oil.

BROWN, Alexander C. (1838-1922) of Edinburgh. Chemist. The rule of substitution for benzine derivatives bears his name.

BROWN, George (1790-1865) from near Elgin. General. Distinguished himself in the Crimea, in the battle of Alma, and at Sebastapol.

BROWN, George Douglas (1869-1902) of Ochiltree, Ayrshire. Novelist son of a farmer. Best remembered for his novel 'The House with the Green Shutters' (1901).

BROWN, John (1722-87) from near Abernethy. Herd-boy and packman who studied philosophy and became a preacher in 1750. He was the author of the 'Self Interpreting Bible'.

BROWN, John (1735-88) of Berwickshire. Physician. Founder of the 'Brunonian' system of medicine.

BROWN, John (1826-83) of Balmoral. For thirty years was personal attendant to Queen Victoria.

BROWN, John, of Paisley. About 1840 with William Polson produced a cornflour powder when they were trying to make starch for cloth from maize. Now Brown and Polson is part of a world-wide concern with a large range of other food products.

BROWN, Sir John D.K., born 1913, educated in Glasgow. President of Bengal Chamber of Commerce and Industry, and Associated Chambers of Commerce of India (1956-60).

BROWN, Robert (1773-1858) of Montrose. Botanist. In 1805 he brought home nearly 4000 species of plants from Australia.

BROWN, Robert (1842-95) of Camster, Caithness. Botanist and geographer. Travelled Greenland, sub-arctic Canada, West Indies and the Barbary States. Wrote 'The Countries of the World', 'Science for All' etc.

BROWN, Sydney, born 1899 in Lanarkshire. Rear Admiral, Extra Naval Assistant to 2nd Sea Lord Engineering personnel (1949-53).

BROWN, William, born 1888 in Dumfriesshire. Emeritus Professor of Plant Pathology, Univ. of London 1953—.

BROWN, Sir William S., born 1890 in Kelso. Secretary to the Board of Revenue (1924-27) and to the Govt. Public Works Dept. Madras (1935-37). Chief Sec. to the Govt. of Madras (1946-47).

BROWNE, John C. McClure, born 1912 in Edinburgh? Appointed Professor of Obstetrics and Gynaecology, University of London in 1952.

BRUCE, Alexander Hugh, 6th Baron Balfour of Burleigh (1849-1921) of Kennet. Statesman. Lord-in-Waiting to Queen Victoria. Sec. Board of Trade (1889-92). One of the most outstanding figures in Scottish public life.

BRUCE, Sir David (1855-1931) of Melbourne, of Scottish descent. Physician and Naturalist. Discovered the causes of Malta fever and sleeping sickness. Elected F.R.S. in 1884.

BRUCE, Fredrick F., born 1910 in Aberdeen. Appointed Professor of Bible Criticism and Exegesis, Univ. of Manchester in 1959.

BRUCE, George Gordon, born 1891 in Tochineal. Surgeon to King George VI and to the Queen (1952-61) in Scotland.

BRUCE, James (1730-94) of Stirlingshire. Explorer in Africa. First Briton to find the source of the Blue Nile. Discovered Tissisat Falls in 1770. His 'Travels to Discover the Source of the Nile' (1790) was published in 5 vols.

BRUCE, Sir John K., born 1905. Surgeon. Lecturer on surgery in the U.S.A. Canada, Australia, England and Copenhagen. Hon. Surgeon to the Queen in Scotland (1960).

BRUCE, ROBERT THE (1274-1329) of Lochmaben or Turnberry. King of Scotland who defeated the English at Bannockburn.

BRUCE, Sir William (? - d. 1710) of Kinross. Architect Royal to Charles II. Rebuilt Holyrood (1671-79).

BRUCE, William Speirs (1867-1921) of Edinburgh? Naturalist, explorer and lecturer on Geography, Oceanography and Zoology. Took part in many polar and other expeditions and surveys in the Antarctic, Waddell Sea and Spitsbergen (1890-1920).

BRUCE LOCKHART, John M., born 1914. Sometime head of Central Staff Dept., Cortaulds Ltd. First Secretary British Embassy in Washington (1951-53).

BRYAN, Sir Andrew, born 1893 in Lanarkshire. Consulting Mining Engineer. Chief Inspector of Mines (1947-51), Member of the National Coal Board (1951-57).

BRYCE, David (1803-76) of Edinburgh. Architect (Scottish Baronial).

BRYCE, G. Robb, born 1921, educ. in Glasgow. Appointed Chief Test Pilot, British Aircraft Corp. in 1960.

BUCHAN, Alexander (1829-1907) from near Kinross. Meteorologist.

Pioneer of the Isobar System.

BUCHAN, John, 1st Baron Tweedsmuir (1875-1940) of Perth. Author and Statesman. Governor of Canada (1935-40).

BUCHAN, William (1729-1805) of Ancarm, Roxburghshire. Physician. Published in 1769 the first edition of 'Domestic Medicine or the Family Physician', the first of its kind in this country.

BUCHANAN, George (1506-82) of Killearn. Historian and tutor to Montaigne, Mary Queen of Scots and James VI.

BUCHANAN, Sir George (1854-1924) Ambassador to Rome (1919), and to Petrograd (1910-17).

BURNES, James (1801-62) of Montrose. Sometime Physician-General of Bombay. Elected F.R.S. in 1834. A relation of Robert Burns.

BURNET, Alastair, born 1928 in Edinburgh. Became editor of 'The Economist' in 1965. Award winner, Guild of TV Producers and Directors (1966). Political Broadcaster of the Year Award 1970.

BURNETT, Sir William (1779-1861) of Montrose. Sometime Physician-General to the Navy. 'Burnett's Fluid', a strong solution of Zinc chloride used as a wood preservative was named after him.

BURNS, Sir George (1795-1890) of Glasgow. Philanthropist and founder of the Cunard Shipping Company with his brother James.

BURNS, Henry S. Mackenzie, born 1900 in Aberdeen. Director of Shell Oil Co. Inc., New York (1947), of U.S. Petroleum Institute (1947-60). Was Vice-Chief of Air Staff (1964-67).

BURNS, James (1789-1871) of Glasgow, brother of Sir George. Co-founder of the Cunard Shipping Company.

BURNS, James, born 1902, educ. Inverness and Cambridge. Chairman Northern Gas Board 1962—. Chief Engineer North Thames Gas Board (1949) and Deputy Chairman (1960-62).

BURNS, Robert (1759-96) of Alloway, near Ayr. Scottish National Bard of world-wide fame. His works are very popular in Russia.

BURNS, William, born 1884 in Montrose. Economic Botanist to the Bombay Govt. (1908); Principal, Poona College of Agriculture (1922-32); Director of Agriculture, Bombay (1932-36) and Agriculture Commissioner to the Govt. of India (1939-43).

BURNS, William, born 1909 in Stonehaven. Professor of Physiology, Charing Cross Hospital Medical School since 1947. Member of the Physiological Society; the Ergonomics Research Society and the British Assoc. for the Advancement of Science.

BURNS, William C. (1815-68) of Forfarshire. Missionary to China. Universally regarded as having been one of the most devoted missionaries since Apostolic times.

BUSBY, Sir Matthew, born 1909. Scottish footballer and football team manager extraordinary. Made Freeman of Manchester in 1967. Affectionately known as 'Matt Busby'.

C

CADELL, Francis (1822-79) of Cockenzie. Explorer in Australia. Explored the Murray river. Was murdered by his crew.

CAIRD, Edward (1835-1908) of Greenock. Idealist and Philosopher. Master of Balliol Coll. Oxford (1893-1907). Best known for his monumental commentary 'The Critical Philosophy of Immanual Kent' (1889).

CAIRD, Rev. George B., born 1917 in Dundee. Principal of Mansfield College, Oxford since 1969.

CAIRD, John (1820-98) of Greenock. Brother of Edward. Preacher and writer. His 'Religion in Common Life' preached before Queen Victoria at Crathie in 1855, was said to have been the greatest single sermon of the century.

CAIRNCROSS, Sir Alexander K., born 1911 in Lesmahago. Economist. Appointed Master of St Peter's Coll. Oxford in 1969.

CALDER, George, born 1894, educ. Edinburgh. Private Secretary to successive Parliamentary Under Secretaries of State (1927-33); Under Sec. Board of Trade (1946); Directing Staff Imperial Defence Coll. (1948); U.K. Commissioner British Phosphate Commissioners (1952-64) and other appointments.

CALDER, James, born 1898, educ. Glasgow. Judge, Supreme Court and Legal Adviser, Tregganu (1938-39). Chief Sec. to Govt. of North Borneo (1946-53) and Acting Governor N. Borneo (1946-52).

CALDER, James Tait (1794-1864) of Castletown, Caithness. Teacher and author of 'The History of Caithness'.

CALDER, James W., born 1914 in Hamilton. Civil Engineer. Chief Inspector of Mines and Quarries since 1970.

CALDER, Sir John A., born 1889. Senior Crown Agent for the Colonies (1943-53).

CALDER, Sir Robert (1745-1818) of Muirtown, Morayshire. Admiral. Was Capt. of the Fleet at the battle of Cape St Vincent.

CALDWELL, Sir Dick, born 1909 in Edinburgh? Surgeon Vice-Admiral. Executive Director Medical Council on Alchoholism. Was Medical Director-General of the Royal Navy (1966-69).

CAMERON, Charles, born in Glasgow. Chemist who in 1820 invented apparatus for producing soda-water.

CAMERON, James, of Dundee. Journalist and author. Granada award Journalist of the Year (1965); Granada award Foreign Correspondent of the Decade (1965) and Hannan Swaffer award winner (1966).

CAMERON, Neil, born 1920, in Perthshire? Air Vice-Marshal. Asst. Chief of Defence Staff (Policy) in 1968. Senior Air Staff Officer, Air Support Command 1970—.

CAMERON, Roderic D., born 1893 in Invernessshire. Major-General, Director of Medical Services, British Army of the Rhine (1950-53).

CAMERON, Thomas W.R., born 1894 in Glasgow. Became Professor of Parasitology at McGill Univ. Montreal. Produced numerous papers on diseases of animals in relation to man.

CAMERON, V. Lovett (1844-94) Scottish explorer in Africa. First to cross Africa from east to west.

CAMPBELL, Angus. In 1889 invented a spindle-type cotton-picking machine.

CAMPBELL, Sir Archibald (1739-91) of Inverneil. General. Sometime Governor of Jamaica and Madras. Buried in Westminster Abbey.

CAMPBELL, Charles A., born 1897, educ. Glasgow. Emeritus Professor of Logic and Rhetoric, Glasgow Univ. since 1961. Was Professor of Philosophy at the Univ. of North Wales, Bangor (1932).

CAMPBELL, Colin (1687-1757) Helped to found the Swedish East

India Company. Made a Noble of Sweden in 1731.

CAMPBELL, Sir Colin (1792-1863) of Glasgow. Commanded the 'Thin Red Line' at Balaclava. Was Commander-in-Chief during the Indian Mutiny. Became a Field Marshal, and is described as the hero of the Indian Mutiny. Made a Freeman of the City of London in 1860.

CAMPBELL, Sir Colin M., 8th Baronet, born 1925 at Dunblane. President of the Federation of Kenya Employers (1962-70); Chairman of the Tea Board of Kenya (1961-67) and of the East African Tea Trade Assoc. (1960-63 and 66-67).

CAMPBELL, Sir David, born 1889, educ. Ayr. Regius Professor of Materia Medica and Theraputics, Univ. of Aberdeen (1930-59); Dean of the Faculty of Medicine (1932-39) and President of the Medical Council (1949-61).

CAMPBELL, Eric (1870-1917). Scottish actor who played the bullying heavy in some of Charlie Chaplin's most famous short films in 1916-17: 'Easy Street', 'The Cure', 'The Adventurer', etc.

CAMPBELL, Ewen, born 1897, educ. Edinburgh and Oxford. Chairman Executive Committee, Scottish Branch Red Cross Soc., Governor of Kordofan Province (1938-47).

CAMPBELL, Ian M., born 1915, educ. Glasgow. Professor of Humanity, Univ. of Edinburgh 1959 —. Professor of Latin, Univ. Coll. of South Wales and Monmouthshire (1954-59).

CAMPBELL, Ian M., born 1922. General Manager, Eastern Region British Rail since 1970.

CAMPBELL, Ian Ross, born of Scottish parents in 1900, educ. Australia. Major-General. Commander of Australian Forces in Korea and Japan (1951-53).

CAMPBELL, John, 1st Baron (1779-1861) of Fifeshire. Legal Biographer, Lord Chief Justice, Lord Chancellor (1859). Inaugurated important legal reforms.

CAMPBELL, John D. Sutherland, 9th Duke of Argyll (1845-1914). Governor-General of Canada (1878-83).

CAMPBELL, Sir John J., born 1897 in Stewarton. General Manager Clydesdale Bank Ltd. (1946-58). President, Institute of Bankers in Scotland (1953-55).

CAMPBELL of Canna, John Lorne, born 1906 in Isle of Canna, Inner Hebrides. Folklorist, editor and author. Published many works in Gaelic.

CAMPBELL, John M., born 1887, educ. Edinburgh and Canada. Dental Historian and Surgeon. Published a number of articles and books on dentistry.

CAMPBELL, Sir Patrick (1773-1841) of Argyllshire. Vice-Admiral, Commander-in-Chief at Cape of Good Hope (1834-37).

CAMPBELL, Robert R., born 1902 in Edinburgh. Artist, writer, lecturer and broadcaster on Art. Director of the National Gallery of South Australia (1951-67).

CAMPBELL, Thomas (1777-1844) of Glasgow. Poet of renown. 'Hohenlinden', 'Ye Mariners of England', and 'The Battle of the Baltic' are among the best known of his poems. He is buried in Westminster Abbey.

CAMPBELL, Thomas (1790-1858) of Edinburgh. Sculptor. Exhibited various works in the Royal Acadamy, London.

CAMPBELL-BANNERMAN, Sir Henry (1836-1908) of Glasgow. Prime Minister of Great Britain (1905-08).

CARGILL, Dame Helen W., of Edinburgh. Air Commandant. Matron-in-Chief Princess Mary's R.A.F. Nursing Service (1948-52).

CARLYLE, Thomas (1795-1881) of Ecclefechan. Writer, essayist and lecturer. Sometime described as a literary genius of the highest order.

CARMICHAEL, Edward A., born 1896 in Edinburgh. Neurologist. Director of Neurological Research Unit, London.

CARMICHAEL, Sir John, born 1910, educ. St Andrews. Chairman Sudan Light and Power (1952-54), Financial and Economic Adviser to Sudan Govt. (1955-59). Chairman Herring Industry Board 1962—.

CARNEGIE, Andrew (1835-1918) of Dunfermline. Iron and Steel works tycoon and philanthropist. Made his vast fortune in America. Said to have given away £100 million. He is reported as having said that it would be a disgrace to die wealthy.

CARNEGIE, William (Lord Northesk). Admiral, third in command to Nelson at Trafalgar, and later became First Sea Lord. Buried in St Pauls beside Nelson and Collingwood.

CAWTHORN, Sir Terence, born 1902 in Aberdeen. Consulting adviser in Otolaryngology to Ministry of Health. Consulting Surgeon, Ear Nose and Throat Dept. King's Coll. Hosp. London, Clinical Director, Wernher Research Unit on Deafness, Medical Research Council.

CHALMERS, James (1782-1853) of Arbroath. Bookseller in Dundee, who invented adhesive stamps, the round one penny stamp.

CHALMERS, William J., born 1914, educ. Inverness. Secretary and Director-General, Commonwealth War Graves Commission 1956—.

CHAMBERS, Robert (1802-1871) of Peebles)
CHAMBERS, William (1800-1883) " ") Brothers, Publishers and founders of the 'Chambers' Journal'.

CHEYNE, James, born 1895, educ. Aberdeen. Administrative Officer in Tanganyika Territory (1918), Provincial Commissioner (1941); Sec. for African Affairs (1948). Member of Local Govt. Tanganyika Territory (1950-51).

CHISHOLM, Sir A. Robert, born 1897. Retired as Managing Director, Imperial Bank of India.

CHISHOLM, Alexander H., born 1890 in Victoria of Scottish parents. Chief Editor Australian Encyclopaedia. Adviser on Fauna and Protection to Queensland Govt. President Royal Australian Historical Society.

CHISHOLM, Eric, born in Glasgow. Composer and Conductor. In 1945 appointed Professor of Music at Cape Town.

CHISHOLM, George, born 1916 in Bridgeton, Glasgow. Musician and funnyman. Once voted Britain's top Jazz trombonist.

CHISHOLM, Ronald G., born 1910 in Inverness. British Deputy High Commissioner to Eastern Nigeria (1963). U.K. Delegate to International Sugar Conference (1953). Deputy High Commissioner for U.K. in Madras (1957-60).

CHRISTISON, Sir Robert (1797-1882) of Edinburgh. Toxicologist and Physician. Wrote a treatise on poisons in 1828. Appointed Physician to Queen Victoria in 1848.

CLAPPERTON, Hugh (1788-1827) of Annan. Explorer in Africa. Died in his attempt to discover the source of the Niger river.

CLAPPERTON, Thomas J. (1879-1962) of Galashiels. Sculptor. 'The

Bruce' at Edinburgh Castle; 'The Border Reiver' in Galashiels; 'Bishop Morgan', Cardiff, and a number of war memorials were his work.

CLARK, Sir Andrew (1826-93) of Wolfhill, near Cupar-Angus. One of the most distinguished doctors of his day. Physician to London Hospital (1854). A great authority on lung diseases.

CLARK, George Aitken (1823-73) of Paisley. Threadmaker (in Paisley and America) and Philanthropist.

CLARK, Sir James (1788-1870) of Cullen. Sometime Physician to Queen Victoria.

CLARK, James (Jim) (1936-68) of Chirnside, Berwickshire. Motor racing driver, twice World Champion. Considered by many, the greatest of all time Grand Prix drivers. Won 25 G.P. races.

CLARKE, Alexander (1828-1914). Geodesist. Remembered for his work on the principal triangulation of the British Isles and for his book 'Geodesy' (1880).

CLERK, John (1728-1812) of Penicuik. Writer on Naval tactics. Published in 1790, fifty copies of his 'Essay on Naval Tactics' and it is believed that Rodney owed his West Indies successes to it.

CLERK-MAXWELL, James (See MAXWELL)

CLUNIES-ROSS, John (c. 1786-1854) of Weisdale, Shetland. Adventurer, sailor and philosopher. Uncrowned King of Cocos Keeling Islands, given to him about 1827, and his descendants, by Queen Victoria.

CLYDE, W. McCallum, born 1901. Professor of English. Became Food Adviser to the Special Commission to S.E. Asia (1946). Leader of the U.K. delegation to U.N.F.A.O. meetings in India, Bangkok, Singapore, Phillipines, Indonesia, Tokio and Rangoon.

COATES, Sir Peter (1808-90) of Paisley.)   Brothers, Industrialists.
COATES, Thomas (1809-83) " ")   Thread manufacturers.

COCHRANE, Sir Ralph, born 1895 in Cults, Aberdeenshire. Air Chief Marshal. Seconded to New Zealand Govt. to advise on air defence. First C-in-C of R.N.Z.A.F. (1936-39). A.D.C. to the King (1939-40). Held various important appointments in Intelligence and Training in the R.A.F.

COCHRANE, Thomas, 10th Earl Dundonald (1775-1860). Admiral. Secured the independence of Chile, Peru and Brazil (1819-25).

COCKBURN, Alicia or Alison (1713-94) of Fairnlee, Selkirkshire. Poetess. Remembered for her poem 'The Flowers of the Forest'. A different poem from the lament for Flodden with the same title by Jean Elliot.

COCKBURN, Henry T. (Lord Cockburn) (1779-1854) of Cockpen or Edinburgh. Judge and author. Shared with Jeffrey the leadership of the Bar. A zealous supporter of parliamentary reform.

COMBE, Andrew (1797-1847) of Edinburgh. Judge and author of several works on Phrenology and Physiological Science. Physician to Queen Victoria (1838).

COMBE, George (1788-1858) of Edinburgh. Brother of Andrew. Eminent Philosopher and author who first introduced Phrenology to Britain. His chief work was 'The Constitution of Man' (1828).

COMFORT, Charles F., born 1900 in Edinburgh. Artist and author. Director of the National Galleries of Canada 1959—.

CONAN DOYLE, Sir Arthur (1859-1930) of Edinburgh. Novelist and writer of detective stories and historical romances. Originator of 'Sherlock Holmes'. Spiritualist.

CONAN DOYLE, Dame Jean, daughter of the late Sir Arthur Conan Doyle. Appointed Director of the Woman's Royal Air Force in 1963.

CONNERY, Sean, born 1930 in Edinburgh. Actor. Star of many great films in the personification of James Bond the Ian Fleming character.

CONWAY, Hugh G., born 1914 in Edinburgh. Managing Director, Rolls Royce Bristol Engine Div. 1964—. Director of Rolls Royce Ltd.

CORBETT, Ronnie, born 1930 in Edinburgh. Actor and comedian. Became popular in 'No that's me over here' and the TV series with Ronnie Barker 'The Two Ronnies'.

CORMACK, James M.R., born 1909 in Aberdeen. Professor of Greek. Lecturer on Classics Univ. of Reading. Dean of the Faculty of Letters (1948-54).

COUTTS, Fredrick, born 1899 in Aberdeenshire. General of the Salvation Army (1963-69).

COUTTS, Thomas (1735-1822) of Edinburgh. Banker. Founder of the London Banking House of Coutts & Co., with his brother James.

CRAIG, William S.R., born 1903. Professor of Paediatrics and child health, Univ. of Leeds. Produced various publications on child and adolescent life in health and disease.

CRAIGIE, James, born 1899, educ. Perth and St Andrews. Member of Scientific Staff, Imperial Cancer Research Fund (1947-64); President Society of American Bacteriologists (1946). Director Mill Hill Laboratories (1949-58).

CRAIK, George Lillie (1798-1866) of Kennoway, Fife. Scholar. In 1849 became Professor of History and English Literature in Queen's Coll. Belfast.

CRAM, Alastair L. (Mr Justice Cram), born 1909, educ. Perth and Edinburgh. Appellate Judge Supreme Court of Appeal, Malawi, (1964-68); Governor-General, Malawi (1965). Athlete, traveller and climber in the Alps, (1930-60), Himalayas (1960), Amazon and Peruvian Andes (1966) and Atlas Mountains (1971).

CRAWFORD, (David R.A. Lindsay) 28th Earl of, born 1900. Premier Earl of Scotland. Deputy Governor, Royal Bank of Scotland (1962—). Chairman British Fine Arts Commission (1943-47).

CRAWFORD, Theodore, born 1911, educ. Glasgow. Professor of Pathology in the Univ. of London 1948—.

CRICHTON, James (1560-82) of Elliock, educ. St Andrews. Renowed for his gifts of learning and general accomplishments. Known as 'The Admirable Crichton'.

CROCKETT, Samuel Rutherford (1860-1914) of Kirkcudbrightshire. Minister and novelist. 'The Men of the Moss Hags' (1895); 'The Grey Men' (1896); 'Kit Kennedy' (1899); 'The Loves of Miss Anne' (1904) and 'The White Plumes of Navarre' (1909) were among his best known works.

CROMBIE, George E., born 1908 in Aberdeen. Counsellor and U.K. High Commissioner, Ottawa (1955-58), British High Commissioner The Gambia (1965-67).

CROMBIE, Sir Harvey F., born 1900 in Aberdeenshire. Rear Admiral (Ret.), Senior Officer Minesweepers, N. Russia (1941-43), Director of Minesweeping (1943-46), Flag Officer, Scotland and Admiral Superintendent, Rosyth (1951-53).

CRONIN, Archibald Joseph, born 1896 in Cardross. Novelist and Playwright. His many successful works include 'Hatter's Castle'; 'The Citadel', and 'The Keys of the Kingdom'.

CRUDEN, Alexander (1701-70) of Aberdeen. Compiled 'Cruden's Biblical Concordance', the first great work of reference in English.

CRUICKSHANK, Andrew J.M., born 1907 in Aberdeen. Actor, famous for his personification of the Dr Cameron of A.J. Cronin.

CRUICKSHANK, Ernest W.H., born 1888 in Edinburgh. Professor of Physiology, Pekin Union Medical College (1920-24), Patna, India (1926-28) and Halifax N.S. (1929-35). Retired as Prof. of Physiology, Marischal Coll. Univ. of Aberdeen (1935-58).

CRUICKSHANK, John, born 1884, educ. Glasgow. Professor of Bacteriology, Aberdeen Univ. (1926-54). Adviser on Pathology to 3rd Army (1917).

CRUICKSHANK, Martin M., born 1888 in Edinburgh. Ophthalmic Specialist in Northern and Western Commands (1921-31); Professor of Surgery, Madras Medical Coll., and Senior Surgeon and Superintendent, General Hospital, Madras (1934-40), Brigadier and Consultant Surgeon, Southern Army India (1943).

CRUICKSHANK, Robert, born 1899 in Aberdeen. Professor of Preventive Medicine, Univ. of West Indies, Kingston (1966-68). Produced various publications on microbiology and immunology etc.

CRUM, Walter Ewing (1865-1944) of Renfrewshire. Coptic scholar. F.B.A. (1931).

CULLEN, William (1710-90) of Hamilton. Physician, to him is largly due the recognition of the important part played by the nervous system in health and disease.

CULLEN, William (1867-1948) of Shettleston, Glasgow. Chemist and Metallurgist, expert on explosives and mining. Spent some time in the mines in South Africa.

CUNNINGHAM, Allan (1784-1842) of Dalswinton, Dumfrieshire. Poet and Man of Letters. His works include 'Traditional Tales of the English and Scottish Peasantry' (1822) and 'The Songs of Scotland Ancient and Modern' (1825) which contains his famous "A wet sheet and a flowing sea".

CUNNINGHAM, Sir Charles, born 1906 in Dundee. Permanent Under-Sec. of State, Home Office (1957-66); Deputy Chief U.K. Atomic Energy Authority (1966-71). Headed Vassel spy inquiry, and Chairman Resettlement Board for Ugandan Asians (1972).

CUNNINGHAM, Sir Charles B., born 1884 in Campbelltown. Com-missioner of Police, Travancore State (1915-21), Madras (1928) and Inspector-General of Police, Madras (1930-38). Inspector of Con-stabulary, Home Office (1940-45).

CUNNINGHAM, William (1849-1919) of Edinburgh. Economist. Taught history at Cambridge and Economics at King's Coll. London.

CURRAN, Samuel C., born 1912, educ. Wishaw and Cambridge. Principal, Royal Coll. of Science and Technology, Glasgow 1959—. Chief Scientist, A.W.R.E., Aldermaston (1958-59).
An authority on the detection of nuclear radiation. Invented the Scintillation Detector and the modern Proportional Counter.

CURRIE, Sir George, born 1896 in Banffshire. Vice-Chancellor Univ. of New Zealand. Principal Research Officer, Council for Scientific and Industrial Research, Australia (1929-39). Published many papers on Scientific Research.

CURRIE, James (1756-1805) of Dumfrieshire. Physician. His chief medical work was the able reports on the effects of water in Fibril diseases (1797).

CURRIE, Sir James, born 1907 in Glasgow. Commercial Counsellor, Washington (1947). Consul-General Copenhagen, San Paulo and Johannesburg (1952-62).

CURRIE, Robert A., born 1905 in Glasgow. Rear Admiral (Ret). Dir-ector R.N. Staff Coll. (1951-52). Chief of Staff to Chairman British Joint Service Mission, Washington (1954-57).

CUTHBERT, Sir John, born 1902 in Glasgow. Vice-Admiral. Com-manded H.M.S. Glasgow (1942); Ajax (1944-46); Vengeance (1949-50). Flag Officer Flotillas, Home Fleet (1953-54). Flag Officer Scotland (1956-58).

CUTHBERTSON, Sir David, born 1900 in Kilmarnock. Consultant Director, Bureau of Animal Nutrition (1945-65). Hon. Consultant in Physiology and Nutrition to the Army (1956-65). Published many papers on physiology of protein nutrition and metabolism etc.

D

DAICHES, David, born 1912 in Edinburgh. Professor of English Univ. of Sussex 1961—. Prof. of English at Cornell Univ. U.S.A. (1946-51). University Lecturer in English at Cambridge (1951-61). Dean of the School of English Studies (1961-68).

DALGETTY, James S., born 1907. Became Senior Legal Draftsman to the Govt. of Nyasaland in 1962.

DALHOUSIE, (James Andrew Broun-Ramsay) Marquis of (1812-60) of Dalhousie Castle. Became the greatest of Indian Proconsuls. Appointed Governor-General of India in 1848, the youngest Viceroy ever, and his administration was a tremendous success.

DALRYMPLE, Alexander (1737-1801) of Musselburgh. Hydrographer of the East India Co. in 1779 and to the Admiralty in 1795.

DALRYMPLE-HAMILTON, Sir Fredrick H.G., born 1890 in Girvin. Vice Admiral Malta and Flag Officer, Central Mediterranean Fleet (1945-46). Admiral British Joint Services Mission Washington D.C. (1948-50).

DALYELL, Tom (1599-1685). Scottish General in the Russian Army. Raised the Royal Scots Greys Regiment in 1681.

DAVIDSON, Charles F., born 1911 in Monifieth. Professor of Geology, Univ. of St Andrews 1955—. Chief Geologist to the British Atomic Energy Organization (1942-55).

DAVIDSON, Rev. D. (1781-1858) of Wick, Caithness. Theologian and editor. Compiler of several Biblical Dictionaries and Commentaries.

DAVIDSON, Francis, born 1905 in Nairn. Finance Officer, Singapore High Commission, London. Sometime Accountant-General to Nigeria.

DAVIDSON, J. Norman, born 1911 in Edinburgh. Professor of Bio-chemistry in Univ. of London, St Thomas's Hosp., (1946-47). Guest lecturer to Ghent, Brussels, Brazil and Malaysia (1954-63) also to Oslo, Upsala, Paris, U.S.A., Warsaw and Moscow.

DAVIDSON, John C. Campbell, Viscount, born 1889 in Aberdeen. Secretary of State for the Colonies (1910); Parliamentary Sec. to the Admiralty (1924-27); Chairman Unionist Party (1927-30). Controller of Production (1941).

DAVIDSON, Randall Thomas, (Lord Davidson of Lambeth) (1857-1909) of Barrhead. Archbishop of Canterbury (1903-28).

DAVIDSON, Roger A. McLaren, born 1900 in Perthshire. In the Colonial Education Service, was Inspector-General of Education, Nigeria (1951-53).

DAVIDSON, Thomas (1840-1900) of Deer, Aberdeenshire. Writer on Mediaeval Philosophy, Rosmini, Education and Art.

DAWSON, John A., born 1910 in Aberdeen. Air Ministry Chief Engineer, Coastal Command Air Defence of Gt. Britain. Director of Works A.M. (1940-48). Chief Resident Engineer London Airport (1948-54).

DENT, Alan H., born 1905 in Ayrshire. Author, critic, journalist and broadcaster. Lectured on fine art criticism at Toronto, Boston, Vassar, Princeton and New York Universities.

DEWAR, Sir James (1842-1923) of Kincardine-on-Forth. Professor at Cambridge. Invented the vacuum flask, discovered cordite, jointly with Sir Fredrick Abel. Liquified and froze many gases, including oxygen.

DEWAR, Kenneth G., born 1879 near Edinburgh. Vice Admiral, Deputy Director Naval Intelligence Div. (1925-27). Commanded H.M.S. Royal Oak and Tiger (1928-29).

DEWAR, Robert J., born 1923 in Glasgow. Chief Conservator of Forests, Nyasaland (1955-60). Director of Forestry and Game, Malawi (1960-64).

DICK, Robert (1811-66) of Tullybody, Clackmannanshire. A baker in Thurso from 1830. Self-taught geologist and botanist.

DICK, Thomas (1774-1857) from near Dundee. Minister and scientist whose astronomical writings tended to support Christian teaching.

DINWIDDIE, Robert (1693-1770). His actual place of birth in Scotland is not certain. Governor of Virginia (1752-58).

DONALD, William, born 1891 in Aberdeen. President The Port Line Ltd., Deputy Chairman Cunard White Star Ltd.; Cunard Steamship Co. Ltd.; Midland Bank Ltd.; Director Cunard House Ltd., and Clydesdale and North of Scotland Bank Ltd. etc.

DONALDSON, David A., born 1916. Artist with paintings in private collections in America and Europe. His sitters have included the Queen.

DOUGALL, Neil (1776-1862) of Greenock. Poet and musical composer. Composed about 100 psalm and hymn tunes including 'Kilmarnock'.

DOUGLAS, Francis C.R. Douglas of Barloch, 1st Baron, born 1889. Educ. Glasgow. Chairman House of Commons and Chairman of Standing Committees (1945-46), of Estimates Cttee. (1945-46) of Finance Cttees of L.C.C. (1940-46). Governor and C-in-C Malta (1946-49).

DOUGLAS, Charles P., born 1921 in Ayr. Professor of Obstetrics and Gynaecology at the Royal Free School of Medicine, London 1965—. Was Senior Lecturer at the Univ. of West Indies (1959-65).

DOUGLAS, David (1798-1834) of Scone. Botanical traveller in North America. Discovered many new species of flora and fauna and introduced to this country many trees and herbaceous plants, including the Douglas fir which bears his name.

DOUGLAS, Gavin, 5th Earl of Angus (c. 1449-1514). Educ. at St Andrews. Poet, nicknamed 'Bell the Cat' from the lead he took against Cochrane of Lauder. He filled the highest offices in State and added largely to the family possessions.

DOUGLAS, Sir James (1803-77). Fur trader known as the Father of British Columbia.

DOUGLAS, William Sholto, 1st Baron Douglas of Kirtleside (1893-1969). Marshal of the Royal Air Force. Sometime Chairman of B.E.A.

DOUGLAS-HOME, Sir Alec, born 1903, Berwickshire. Foreign Secretary. Prime Minister of Gt. Britain in 1963.

DOWDING, Hugh C.T., 1st Baron (1882-1970) of Moffat. Air Chief Marshal, Royal Air Force. Chief of Fighter Command in the 'Battle of Britain'.

DOWIE, John Alexander (1847-1907) of Edinburgh. Minister and faith healer, calling himself 'Elijah the Restorer'. Founded, near Chicago the prosperous industrial and banking community called 'Zion City'.

DOWNIE, Allan W., born 1901 in Rosehearty. Professor of Bacteriology, Liverpool Univ. (1943-66).

DRENNAN, Alexander M., born 1884 in Helensburgh. Professor of Pathology, Otago Univ., Dunedin (1914-28) and Queen's Coll. Belfast (1928-31).

DREVER, James, born 1910 in Edinburgh? Professor and lecturer on Psychology and Philosophy, King's Coll. Newcastle-upon-Tyne (1938 -41); Royal Navy (1941-45); President Brit. Psychological Society (1960-61) and Social Research Council 1965—.

DRUMMOND, Sir Alexander, born 1901 in Dundee. Lieut.-General, Director-General Army Medical Services (1956-61).

DRUMMOND, Dame Edith Margaret, born in Glasgow? Director of the Women's Royal Naval Service (1964-67).

DRUMMOND, Henry (1851-97) of Stirling. Scientist and writer. Made geological surveys in the Rocky Mountains and Central Africa. His chief contribution to literature was his 'Natural Law in the Spiritual World' (1883).

DRUMMOND, James Eric, 16th Earl of Perth (1876-1951). First Secretary-General of the League of Nations (1919-32).

DRUMMOND, Thomas (1797-1840) of Edinburgh. Engineer and Statesman. Invented 'Limelight'. Became head of the Boundry Commission under the Reform Bill. Under-Sec. for Ireland (1835).

DRUMMOND, William (1585-1649) of Hawthornden, Midlothian. Man of Letters and Poet, mainly on political matters. Ben Johnson walked from London to Scotland to pay him tribute.

DUFF, Alexander (1806-78) from near Pitlochry. Ordained first Scottish missionary to India. One of the founders of the University of Calcutta.

DUFF, Sir Mountstuart E. Grant (1829-1906) of Aberdeenshire. Diarist. Was Governor of Madras till 1886. Elected F.R.S.

DUFF, Sir Robert William (1835-95) of Banffshire. Man of Letters. Became Governor of New South Wales, Australia.

DUGUID, David R., born 1888 in Boness. Major-General, Engineering. Director of Mechanical Engineering, India, and head of the Corps of Indian Electrical and Mechanical Engineering (1943-46).

DUGUID, John B., born 1895 in Belhelvie, Aberdeenshire. Lecturer in Morbid Anatomy and History. Adviser on Histopathology to the

Institute for Medical Research, Kuala Lampur, Malaya (1960-68).

DUKE-ELDER, Sir Stewart, St Andrews' First Foundation Scholar (1915). Ophthalmic surgeon of world renown.

DUNBAR, Claud I.H., born 1909 in Aviemore? Major-General. Commanded 2nd Guards Brigade (1949-50) and 4th Gds. Bde. (1950-52). General Officer Commanding Berlin (British Sector) 1962—.

DUNBAR-NASMITH, David, born 1921 in Glenrothes. Rear Admiral, Retired in 1972 as Flag Officer Scotland and Northern Ireland, and several N.A.T.O. appointments.

DUNCAN, Adam (1731-1804) of Dundee. When Admiral in command of the North Sea Fleet he blockaded the Dutch Fleet for two years. Victor of the battle of Camperdown in 1797.

DUNCAN, David, born 1900 in Dumfries. Surgeon Rear Admiral. Malariaologist and Hygienist, Singapore (1930-38). Senior M.O., Medical Hygiene Sections and Naval Medical Officer of Health to C-in-C, Nore (1950-53). M.O.H. to C-in-C, Portsmouth (1953-55).

DUNDAS, David (1735-1820). Scottish General, sometime Commander-in-Chief, British Army. Described as the profoundest tactician in England. Was responsible for many major reforms in military tactics.

DUNDAS, 1st Viscount Melville and Baron Dunira (1742-1811). Parliamentarian. Keeper of the Signet for Scotland in 1777. As President of the Board of Control under Pitt he introduced a bill for restoring the Scottish estates forfeited after the '45.

DUNDAS, Sir Robert, born 1881 in Perthshire. Administration Officer, Nigeria (1911-30).

DUNDAS, Sir Thomas, born 1906. Director of Barclay's bank (1954-67).

DUNDEE, John Graham of Claverhouse, 1st Viscount (1649-89). Soldier. Defeated the Covenanters at Bothwell Brig. Known by his friends as 'Bonnie Dundee' and by his enemies as 'Bloody Claverse'.

DUNDONALD, Thomas Cochrane, 10th Earl of Dundonald (1775-1860) of Hamilton. Seaman and Naval commander with some remarkable achievements in the harassment of enemy coasts and shipping. He advocated steam power for warships. His 'Secret War Plan' (to overwhelm fleets and fortresses by sulphur fumes) was in 1812 and in 1846 condemned as too inhuman, though infallable, and was not revealed till 1908 (in Penmure Papers).

DUNLOP, John Boyd (1840-1921) of Dreghorn, Ayrshire. Veterinary surgeon. Invented the pneumatic tyre in 1888.

DUNN, Patrick H., born 1912 in Argyleshire. Air Marshal. A.O.C-in-C, Flying Training Command 1964—.

DUNNE, J.W., of Perthshire, Man of Letters. In 1907, tested the first swept-wing tailless biplane at Blair Atholl.

DUNNETT, Alastair, born 1908 in Kilmalcolm. Journalist and editor of the 'Daily Record' (1946-55) and 'Scotsman' 1956—.

DUNNETT, Sir James, born 1914 in Edinburgh? Permanent Under-Secretary of State, Ministry of Defence, 1966—.

DUNS-SCOTUS, Johannes (c.1265-1308) of Maxton, Roxburgh. Scholastic. Became a Franciscan Friar. Theological professor at Oxford, and later, Regent of the University of Paris. It was his name that gave rise to the term 'Dunce'.

DUTHIE, Sir William, born 1892 in Portessie, Banffshire. Appointed Area Bread Officer, London and S.E. England (1940) and Director Emergency Bread Supplies, Min. of Food (1941).

DYCE, Alexander (1798-1869) of Edinburgh. Critic and Man of Letters. Edited Peele, Webster, Greene, Shirley, Middleton, Beaumont and Fletcher, Marlowe and Shakespeare.

DYCE, William (1806-64) of Aberdeen. Historical and religious painter. From 1844, Professor of Fine Arts in King's Coll. London. Executed frescoes in the new House of Lords, Osborne House, Buckingham Palace and All Saints.

DYSON, Sir Frank (1868-1939). Astronomer Royal (1910-33). Previously Astronomer Royal for Scotland (1905-10).

E

EADIE, John (1810-76) of Alva. Theologian and writer. Wrote the 'Biblical Cyclopaedia' (1848), and 'Ecclesiastical Encyclopaedia' (1861)

ELGIN, (Thomas Bruce), 7th Earl of Elgin (1766-1841). Diplomat and art connoisseur. Was instrumental in the purchase for the nation of sculptures from the ruined Parthenon in Athens, now known as the 'Elgin Marbles'.

ELGIN, (James Bruce), 8th Earl of Elgin (1811-63). Governor of Jamaica (1842-46); of Canada (1846-54) and of India (1861). Displayed great administrative ability.

ELGIN, (Edward James Bruce) 10th Earl of Elgin and Kincardine (1881-1966). Was Chairman Standing Council of Scottish Chiefs. Held many Directorships in Banking and Insurance. Chairman Land Settlement Assoc., England and Wales (1933-46), Carnegie U.K. Trust (1923-46) and Forth Conservancy Board (1926-55).

ELGIN, (Andrew Douglas A.T. Bruce), 11th Earl of Elgin and Kincardine. Director United Dominions Trust; Dominion Ins. Co. and several other Companies. Grand Master Mason for Scotland (1961-65). Member of H.M. Body Guard for Scotland, (The Royal Company of Archers).

ELIOT LOCKHART, Sir Allan, born 1905 in Cleghorn. Head of Dept. of Supply, Govt. of India (1940-46); Director-General of Munitions Production (1945-46). President, Assoc. Chamber of Commerce and Bengal Chamber of Commerce and Industry (1951-52).

ELIZABETH, (Lady Elizabeth Angela Margurite Bowes-Lyon) of Glamis Castle, Nr. Forfar, Angus.   Her Majesty Queen Elizabeth the Queen Mother.

ELLIOT, George Augustus, 1st Baron Heathfield of Stobs, Roxburgh-shire. Governor of Gibraltar, who saved the Rock for Britain after four years siege by the French and Spanish forces (1779-83). Ranked as one of the most memorable achievements of British arms.

ELLIOT, Gilbert, 1st Earl Minto (1751-1814).   One of the greatest of India's Governor-Generals.

ELLIOT, Henry H., born 1891 in Roxburghshire. Lieut.-Colonel. and Surgeon, British Legation, Kabul, (1930-35); Surgeon to the Viceroy (1936-43) and Chief Medical Officer, Baluchistan (1944).

ELLIOT, Jean (1727-1805) of Teviotdale. Lyricist. Author of 'The Flowers of the Forest', a lament for Flodden.

ELLIOT, Walter (1888-1958). Politician, writer and broadcaster. Minister of Agriculture (1932-36); Secretary for Scotland (1936-38) and Minister of Health (1938-40).

ELPHINSTONE, George Keith (1746-1823) Viscount Keith of Stirling. Commanded the Naval expedition (1795-97) which took Cape Town, and the fleet which landed Abercromby's army in Aboukir Bay in 1801.

ELPHINSTONE, Sir Keith (1864-1941) of Musselburgh. Engineer, who between 1893 and 1914 was connected with the development and invention of many electrical and mechanical devices. He designed the first chart recorder, and invented the speedometer for motor cars.

ELPHINSTONE, Mountstuart (1779-1859), educ. Edinburgh. Statesman and historian. Governor of Bombay (1819-27). In 1829 he declined the position of Governor-General of India.

ELPHINSTONE, William (1431-1514) of Glasgow. Statesman. Lecturer on law in Paris and Orleans. Ambassador to France under James IV (1491) and keeper of the Privy Seal from 1492.

EMERY, Eleanor, of Glasgow. Diplomat. Appointed High Commissioner in Botswana in 1973. Britain's first woman High Commissioner.

ERROL of HALE, (Fredrick James Elliot) born 1914. Engineer. Economic Sec. to the Treasury (1958-59); Minister of State, Board of Trade (1959-61); President, Board of Trade (1961-63); Minister of Power (1963-64), and many other important appointments at home and abroad.

ERSKINE of RERRICK, (John Maxwell Erskine) 1st Baron, born 1893, in Kirkcudbright. Governor of Northern Ireland (1964-68). President Scottish Savings Committee (1948-58). Several Chairmanships in Banking and Commerce.

ERSKINE, Henry (1746-1817) of Edinburgh. Jurist, writer, orator and wit. Became Lord Advocate (1783) and Dean of the Faculty of Advocates (1785), but was deposed in 1796 for supporting, at a meeting, a resolution against the Government's Seditious Writings Bill. Was again Lord Advocate in 1806.

ERSKINE, Ralph (1685-1752) probably of Berwickshire. Minister who's sermons were greatly prized, and many of them were translated into Dutch. His 'Gospel Sonnets' and 'Scripture Songs' are well known.

ERSKINE, Thomas, 1st Baron (1749-1828) of Edinburgh. Lord Chancellor of England. Called to the Bar in 1778, and his success was immediate and unprecedented. His brilliant defence (1778) of Capt. Baillie, Lieut.-Governor of Greenwich Hosp., who was threatened with a criminal prosecution for libel, overwhelmed him with briefs. He successfully defended (1779) Admiral Lord Keppel and in 1781 secured the acquittal of Lord George Gordon.

EWART, James C. (1851-1933) of Penicuik. Zoologist. Carried out notable experiments on animal breeding and hybridization, and disproved the theory of telegony.

EWING, Sir Alexander, born 1896 in Edinburgh? Emeritus Professor of Audiology and Education of the deaf (1944-46) Manchester. Produced many publications on the education and training of deaf children.

EWING, Sir James Alfred (1855-1935) of Dundee. Professor of Engineering at Tokio and Dundee, of Mechanism at Cambridge (1890 -1903), and Director of Naval Education (1903-16). In World War I, was decipherer of intercepted messages.

F

FAIRBAIRN, Andrew Martin (1834-1912) of Inverkeithing. Theologian, known for his brilliant essays in the 'Contemporary Review' and his 'Studies in the Philosophy of Religion in History' (1876).

FAIRBAIRN, Sir William (1789-1874) of Kelso. Mechanical Engineer and inventor. First in the utilization of iron in shipbuilding. Devised a riveting machine and built bridges (nearly 1000). Elected F.R.S. in 1850.

FALCONER, Hugh (1808-65) of Forres. Botanist. Made the first experiments in growing tea in India. Became Professor of Botany at Calcutta in 1847.

FALCONER, Ion Keith (1856-87) third son of the Earl of Kintore. Orientalist, missionary and athlete. A keen cyclist, he defeated the then (1878) fastest rider in the world. Was Professor of Arabic at Cambridge. He had settled at Shaikh Othman, near Aden as a Free Church missionary when he died of a fever.

FALCONER, William (1732-69) of Edinburgh. Poet. Wrote 'The Ship-wreck', a stirring poem of his experiences on an East Indiaman.

FARQUHARSON, David (1840-1907) of Blairgowrie. Painter, who specialized in landscapes of the Scottish Highlands and Cornish Coast.

FARQUHARSON, Sir James, born 1903 in Angus. Chief Engineer Tanganyika Railways (1941-45) and General Manager (1945-48), and many other important posts in East Africa.

FERGUSON, Adam (1723-1816) of Perthshire. Philosopher and historian. Professor of Mathematics and Moral Philosophy at Edinburgh Univ. (1764-85). His principal works incl. 'Essays on the History of Civil Society' (1765) and 'History of the progress and termination of the Roman Republic' (1782). Sir Walter Scott was his intimate friend.

FERGUSON, James (1710-76) of Rothiemay, Banffshire. Eminent scientific lecturer, astronomer and portrait painter. F.R.S.

FERGUSON, Patrick (1744-80) of Pitfour, Aberdeenshire. Inventor of a breech loading rifle. In 1776 he patented his rifle, firing seven shots a minute and sighted for ranges 100 to 500 yards.

FERGUSON. Robert (1637-1714) of Alford, Aberdeenshire. Called 'The Plotter', he played, for ten years, a leading part in every treasonable scheme against the last two Stuart Kings.

FERGUSON, William A., born 1902 in Glasgow. Secretary British Museum (Natural History) 1959—. Finance Officer, British Museums (1953-59).

FERGUSSON, Sir Bernard, born 1911. Brigadier and wartime Chindit Leader. Director Combined Operations (1945-6). Governor-General of New Zealand (1962-67).

FERGUSSON, Sir Ewan, born 1897, educ. Coatbridge. Chairman and Managing Director, the Straits Trading Co. Ltd., Singapore, 1947—. Chairman Singapore Chamber of Commerce (1946-53).

FERGUSSON, James (1808-86) of Ayr. Art historian. Studied Indian rock temples, wrote on fortifications and archaeology. Author of a popular 'History of Architecture' (1865-67), and a book on the use of earthworks in fortifications.

FERGUSSON, Sir James (1832-1907) of Edinburgh. Statesman. Governor of South Australia (1868-73); of New Zealand (1873-74) and of Bombay (1880-85). He perished in the earthquake of 1907 at Kingston, Jamaica.

FERGUSSON, Sir William (1808-77) of Prestonpans. Surgeon. President of the Royal Coll, of Surgeons, London (1870). F.R.S.

FERRIER, Sir David (1843-1928) of Aberdeen. Neurologist. Joined the staff of King's Coll. London where he was appointed to the specially created Chair of Neurothology in 1887. Best known for his work on the localization of brain functions, on which he was ahead of his time.

FERRIER, John (1761-1815) from near Jedburgh. Poet, Doctor and Critic. At Manchester, where he became a doctor to the Infirmary, he campaigned for better sanitary laws.

FERRIER, Susan Edmonstone (1782-1854) of Edinburgh. Novelist. Her first work 'Marriage' (1818) was followed by 'The Inheritance' (1824) and 'Destiny' (1831).

FERRIER, Victor, 1st Baron of Culter (life peer), born 1900 in Edinburgh. Sometime Director, Imperial Bank of India, and President Bombay Chamber of Commerce.

FETTES, Sir William (1750-1836).   Founder of Fettes College, Edinburgh.

FIFE or Phyfe, Sir Duncan. Scottish cabinetmaker who became famous in America.

FINDLATER, Andrew (1810-85) of Aberdour. Editor. Edited the first edition of Chamber's Encyclopaedia (1860-68). Wrote Manuals on Astronomy, Philology, Physical geography and Physiography.

FINDLAY, Alexander, born 1874. Professor Emeritus of Chemistry. Was examiner in Chemistry at Univ's. of Aberdeen, Durham, London, Wales, St Andrews and New Zealand. Visited India and S. Africa on behalf of the Royal Institute of Chemistry (1947-48).

FINDLAY, Alexander J., born 1886 in Aberdeen. Director of Agriculture, Zanzibar (1931-37). Commissioner for the Colonial Exhibition, World's Fair New York (1939-40).

FINLAY, Robert B., Viscount (1842-1929) of Edinburgh. Called to the English Bar in 1867. Became Solicitor-General (1895-1900); Attorny General (1900-06); Lord Chancellor (1916-19) and in 1920, appointed member of the Hague Permanent Court of Arbitration.

FINLAYSON, Horace, born 1885 in Aberdeen. Professor of Politics and Public Administration, Chinese Govt. Univ. Peking (1910). Technical Adviser to the Bank of Greece under League of Nations Reconstruction Scheme (1928-37). In Financial Intelligence Branch, Ministry of Economic Warfare (1939-45).

FINLAYSON, John (1783-1860) of Caithness. Became a Govt. Calculator and Actuary of the National Debt Office, London.

FISHER, Andrew (1862-1929) of Kilmarnock. Prime Minister of Australia (1908-09) and (1910-13).

FLECK, Sir Alexander, born 1889 in Glasgow. Industrialist. By 1931 was Managing Director of the General Chemical Div. of the Imperial Chemical Industry. During World War II his main responsibility was to maintain supplies of explosives. Became Chairman I.C.I. in 1953. Elected F.R.S. in 1955.

FLEMING, Sir Alexander (1881-1955) of Lochfield, Ayrshire. Bacteriologist. Discovered Penicillin in 1928. Elected F.R.S. in 1943.

FLEMING, John M., born 1911 in Bathgate. Economist. Visiting Professor Columbia Univ. New York (1951-54). Adviser, International Monetary Fund (1959) and Deputy Director, Research Dept. International Monetary Fund 1964—.

FLEMING, Sir Sandford (1827-1915) of Kirkcaldy. Canadian Engineer. Took a prominent part in railway development in upper Canada. Chief Engineer, Northern Railways (1855-63).

FLETCHER, Andrew (1655-1716) of East Lothian. Statesman and political writer. He opposed the union of the crowns and advocated federation rather than incorporation. He introduced various improvements in agriculture. Was noted for his saying "Give me the making of the songs of a nation, and I care not who makes its laws" which occurs in his 'Conversation concerning a Right Regulation of Government for the Common Good of Mankind' (1703).

FORBES, Archibald (1838-1900). Scottish War Correspondent for 'The Daily News' in the Franco/Russian War, the Carlist revolt, the Russo/Turkish campaign and the Zulu war.

FORBES, Sir Archibald, born 1903 in Johnstone, Renfrewshire. Chairman Midland Bank Ltd. and Midland International Bank Ltd. 1964—. Vice President British Banker's Assoc. 1969.

FORBES, Sir Douglas, born 1890 in Aberdeen. Director, National Bank of Australia Ltd. (1948-67).

FORBES, Gilbert, born 1908 in Glasgow. Regius Professor of Forensic Medicine. Senior Lecturer on Forensic Medicine Univ. of Sheffield (1948-56). Examiner in Forensic Medicine Univ's. of Manchester, Leeds, Glasgow, Aberdeen and Edinburgh.

FORBES, James D., (1809-68) of Edinburgh. Scientist and writer. Was one of the founders of the British Association in 1831. His investigations and discoveries embraced the subjects of heat, light polarization and especially glaciers.

FORBES, Sir John (1787-1861) of Cuttlebrae, Banffshire. Physician. Was joint editor of the 'Cyclopaedia of Practical Medicine' (1832-35). Translated the works of Auenbrugger and Laennec and thus advocated the use of the stethoscope in this country.

FORDOUN, John of (died 1384) of Fourdoun. Is the chief authority for Scottish history before 1400.

FORREST, John S., born 1909 in Hamilton. Founder and Director Central Electricity Research Laboratories, Leatherhead (1940).

FORRESTER, Charles, born Edinburgh. Scientific consultant. Professor of Chemistry, Indian School of Mines (1926); Scientific Officer of the British Coal Utilisation Research Assoc. (1960-63). Held many important posts in India in fuel research.

FORSYTH, Alexander John (1768-1843) of Belhelvie, Aberdeenshire. Inventor and Clergyman. In 1807 patented his application of the detonating principal in firearms, which was followed by the adaption of the percussion cap. He was pensioned by the British Govt. after refusing to sell the secret to Napoleon.

FORSYTH, Andrew (1858-1942) of Glasgow. Mathematician and lecturer. By 1890 was recognized as the most brilliant pure Mathematician in the British Empire.

FORSYTH, Ian M., born 1892 in Anstruther. U.K. Delegate to the European Coal Organization (1946-47). Under-Sec. Ministry of Fuel and Power (1946-52).

FORSYTH, William (1737-1804) of Old Meldrum. Gardener who became, in 1784, Superintendent of the Royal Gardens of St James and Kensington. Published several works on diseases etc. in fruit. The shrub 'Forsythia' bears his name.

FORTUNE, Robert (1813-80) of Berwickshire. Botanist. Travelled, extensively in the East, for the London Botanical Society, and introduced many oriental plants into Britain.

FRASER, Alexander (1827-99). Scottish landscape painter.

FRASER, Bill, born 1907. Comic Character Actor. Played many parts in Films and on TV.

FRASER, Francis C., born 1903 in Dingwell. Keeper of Zoology, Brit. Museum (Natural History) 1957—. Took part in 'Discovery' investigations (1925-33), and Danish 'Atlantide' expedition West Africa (1945-46).

FRASER, Sir Hugh, born 1936, in Glasgow ? Chairman since 1966 of 'The House of Fraser' which incorporates 'Harrods'.

FRASER, James Baillie (1783-1856) of Inverness-shire. Traveller, Man of Letters and Explorer. Explored in the Himalayas and travelled extensively in India and Persia.

FRASER, John (1750-1811) of Inverness-shire. Botanist. Introduced many plants to Britain from America and Cuba. Was Botanical Collector to the Czar of Russia (1797-98).

FRASER, Sir Malcolm. Colonial Secretary for West Australia (1883-90), and Agent-General for W. Australia in 1892.

FRASER, Peter (1884-1950) of Fearn, Ross and Cromarty. Labour Prime Minister of New Zealand (1940-49).

FRASER, Simon, Scottish explorer in North West Canada. Fraser river is named after him. He was the first to descend the river to the sea in 1808.

FRASER, Thomas C., born 1909 in Aberdeen. Director, Commission of Inquiry into Industrial Relations 1970. Chairman Economic Development Committee for wool textile industry 1971—.

FRASER, Sir Thomas Richard (1841-1920), born in Calcutta of Scottish parents. Pharmacologist. Chairman, Indian Plague Commission, (1891-1901). President of the Assoc. of Physicians of Gt. Britain and Ireland, (1908-09).

FRASER, Hon Lord, (Walter I.R. Fraser), born 1911 in Glasgow. One of the Senators of H.M. College of Justice in Scotland, 1964. Member of the Queen's Body Guard for Scotland (Royal Company of Archers).

FRASER-DARLING, Sir Frank, born 1903, educ. Edinburgh. President Conservation Foundation Washington D.C. Hon. Trustee, National Parks of Kenya. Member, Royal Commission on Environmental Pollution 1970—.

FRAZER, Sir James George (1854-1941) of Glasgow. Social Anthropologist and Folklorist. Appointed Professor of Social Anthropology at Liverpool in 1907. Author of 'The Golden Bough' (12 vols.).

FULTON, Sir John Scott, born 1902 in Dundee. Vice-Chancellor Univ. of Sussex 1959—. Principal Univ. Coll. Swansea (1947-59); Chairman, Commission on educational requirements of Sierra Leone (1954) and the B.B.C. and I.T.A. Liaison Advisory Committee on Adult Educational Programmes 1962—.

FYFE, Sir William H., born 1878 educ. Edinburgh and Oxford. Principal and Vice-Chancellor of Queen's Univ. Kingston, Ontario (1930-36) and of the Univ. of Aberdeen (1936-48).

FYFFE, Will (1885-1947) of Dundee. Music-hall Comedian. Considered one of the best pantomime comedians of his day.

G

GALLOWAY, Sir Alexander, born 1895, in Dunbar. High Commissioner and Commander-in-Chief, British troops, Austria (1947-50). Chairman Jordan Development Bank (1951-52).

GALLOWAY, Sir Archibald (1780-1850) of Perth. Major General and writer on India.

GALLOWAY, Thomas (1796-1851) of Symington. Mathematician, Astronomer and writer.

GALT, John (1779-1839) of Irvine. Novelist. His best work includes 'The Steamboat'; 'The Provost' and 'Sir Andrew Wylie' (1822), and 'The Entail' (1824). His biographical works included 'Life of Byron' (1830). He founded the Canada Company, a commercial enterprise that was disappointing. The town of Galt in Canada is named after him.

GEAR, William, born 1915 in Methil. Painter. Head of the Faculty of Fine Art and Design, Birmingham 1964—. Has works in permanent collections in many parts of the world.

GED, William (1690-1749) of Edinburgh. Painter. Invented a process of stereotyping in 1725.

GEDDES, Sir A. Reay, born 1912, son of Sir Eric Geddes, of Scottish descent. Chairman of Dunlop Rubber Co. 1968—.

GEDDES, Alexander (1737-1802) of Ruthven, Banffshire. Theologian, Bible critic and writer. Made a new translation of the bible for Catholics (1792-1800). He was also a poet.

GEDDES, Andrew (1783-1844) of Edinburgh. Painter and Etcher.

GEDDES, Sir Auckland Campbell, 1st Baron (1897-1954) Surgeon, Soldier, Professor of Anatomy, Cabinet Minister and Ambassador. Sometime Chairman of the Dunlop Rubber Co., and first Chairman Imperial Airways Co. in 1924. British Ambassador to Washington (1920-24).

GEDDES, Sir Eric (1875-1937), born in Agra, India of Scottish parents, brother of Sir Auckland. Presided over, what became known as 'The Geddes Axe' committee on National expenditure. Was Director-General of Military Railways (1916-17), and Vice-Admiral and First Lord of the Admiralty (1917). A man of tremendous drive and ability.

GEDDES, Ford Irvine, born 1913, of Scottish descent. Chairman British Shipping Federation (1965-68); and of P & O Steam Navigation Co. (1971-72).

GEDDES, Jenny, born in Edinburgh. In 1637, in St Giles she threw a stool at the Dean after the introduction of Land's new prayer book, and shouted, "Thou false thief, dost thou daur say mass at my lug".

GEDDES, Sir Patrick (1854-1932) of Ballater. Has been described as the Father of modern town planning and 50 years ahead of his time.

GEDDES, Ross Campbell, 2nd Baron, born 1907. Chairman, British Travel Assoc. since 1964, and other Directorships and Chairmanships in Shipping.

GEDDIE, John L., born 1881 in Edinburgh. Lecteur d'Anglais at Univ. of Lyons (1903-04) and at Sarboune, Paris (1905-06), Editor Chamber's Journal (1915-47).

GEIKLE, Sir Archibald (1835-1924) of Edinburgh. Geologist. Was (1882-1901) Director-General of the survey of the U.K. and head of the Geological Museum, London. President of the Royal Society (1908-13).

GEIKLE, James (1839-1915) of Edinburgh. Geologist. Wrote a standard work on the Glacial period (1874) and several other geological books.

GEMMELL, Andrew R., born 1913 in Ayrshire? Professor of Biology,

Univ. of Keele since 1950. Lecturer and regular broadcaster, since 1950, with the B.B.C. in 'Gardener's Question Time'.

GEORGE, Sir Robert A., born 1897, son of the late Wm. George of Invergordon. Air Vice-Marshal, Air Attaché, Turkey, Greece and R.A.F. Middle East (1939-44). Governor of Southern Australia (1953-60).

GIBBON, Louis Grassic (1901-1935) of Aberdeenshire. Novelist. His real name, James Leslie Mitchell. His 'Sunset Song' (1932); 'Cloud Home' (1933); and 'Grey Granite' (1934) were very popular.

GIBBS, James (1682-1754) of Aberdeen. Architect. St Martin-in-the-Fields and Radcliffe Camera Library at Oxford (1737-47) are two of the fine buildings designed by him. His 'Book of Architecture' (1728) helped to spread the Palladian style and influenced the design of many churches in America. He was a friend of Wren.

GIBSON, Alexander (1800-67) of Laurencekirk. Botanist. Became, in 1838, Superintendent of the botanical gardens at Dupuri, India, and Conservator of Forests in Bombay (1847-61).

GIBSON, Alexander, born in Motherwell. Conductor and Musical Director, Scottish National Orchestra, 1959—. Musical Director Sadler's Wells Opera (1954-57).

GIFFIN, Sir Robert (1837-1910) of Strathaven. Journalist, economist and statistician. Sometimes Comptroller-General of the Commercial Labour and Statistical Dept. of the Board of Trade.

GILCHRIST, Sir Andrew, born 1910 in Lesmahagow. Ambassador to the Republic of Ireland (1967); Under-Sec. of State, Commonwealth (1966-67) and Consul-General at Chicago (1960-62). Chairman Highlands and Islands Development Bd., 1970—.

GILCHRIST, Rae, born 1899 in Edinburgh. Consulting physician and lecturer on disorders of the heart and circulation. Lectured in England, America and Africa.

GILCHRIST, Robert N., born 1888 in Aberdeen. Held many high posts in the Indian Educational Service (1910-37).

GILL, Sir David (1843-1914) of Aberdeen. Astronomer at the Cape Observatory (1879-1907). Pioneered the use of photography as a means of charting the heavens.

GILLESPIE, Dame Helen, born 1898 in Edinburgh. Brigadier, Matron-in-Chief and Director of the Army Nursing Services, War Office (1952-56).

GILLIES, John (1747-1836) of Brechin. Historian. Appointed Historiographer Royal for Scotland in 1793. His writings include a 'History of Greece' (1786) and a 'History of the World from Alexander to Augustus' (1807).

GILLIES, Marshall M., born 1901 in Lesmahagow. Sometime Professor of Classics at the University of Hull.

GILMOUR, Andrew, born 1898 in Burntisland. Shipping Controller Singapore (1939-41); Defence Intelligence Officer Hong Kong (1941) and Planning Economist U.N. Technical Assistance Mission to Cambodia (1953-55).

GLAISTER, John, born 1892 in Glasgow. Emeritus Professor of Forensic medicine at the Univ. of Egypt, Cairo, and Medical and Legal Consultant to the Govt. of Egypt (1928-32). External examiner in Forensic medicine at the univ's. of Edinburgh, Birmingham, Liverpool, Leeds, Aberdeen, St Andrews and Sheffield.

GLEIG, George Robert (1796-1888) of Stirling. Novelist and biographer. Took Orders in 1820 and became Chaplain-General of the Army (1844) and Inspector-General of Military Schools in 1846.

GLEN, Sir Alexander, born 1912 in Glasgow. Chairman, British Tourist Auth. 1969—. Leader of Oxford Univ. Arctic Expedition (1935-36). Holder of several British and foreign awards for Anthropology and Geography.

GOODSIR, John (1814-67) of Anstruther. Anatomist. Best known for his work in Cellular Pathology.

GORDON, Alexander (1669-1751) of Auchintoul. Was a General in the Russian Army for many years.

GORDON, Sir Archibald M., born 1892 in Seaton Lodge. Barrister-at-Law, Counsellor and Labour Attaché, British Embassy, Washington D.C. (1942). President U.N. League of Lawyers (1956).

GORDON, Charles George (1833-85). Descended from the House of Huntly. General Gordon of Khartoum.

GORDON, Donald, born 1901 in Old Meldrum. Chairman and President, Canadian National Railways 1950—. Sometime Director Trans-Canadian Airlines. Was Deputy Governor, Bank of Canada (1938).

GORDON, Hugh W., born 1897 in Dumfries. Professor and Consulting Physician to Dept. of Skin Diseases, St George's Hosp. Consulting Dermatologist to Royal Marsden Hosp. and West London Hospital.

GORDON, Ian A., born 1908 in Edinburgh. Professor of English language and literature, Wellington Univ. New Zealand 1936—.

GORDON, Sir James Alexander (1782-1869). Sometime Admiral of the Fleet.

GORDON, Sir John Watson (1788-1864) of Edinburgh. Portrait Painter. R.A. (1851).

GORDON, John Rutherford, born 1890 in Dundee? Sometime Editor-in-Chief Sunday Express and Trustee of Beaverbrook Foundation. President Institute of Journalists (1948-49).

GORDON, Patrick (1635-99) of Aberdeenshire. Soldier of fortune, became a General in the Russian Army in 1688.

GORDON, Percival H., born 1884 in Craigmyle. Judge of Court of Appeal, Saskatchewan (1934-61).

GORDON, Sir Robert (1647-1704) of Gordonstoun. Inventor and reputed warlock. Designed a pump for raising water.

GORDON, Thomas, Father of the Russian Navy. Made an Admiral by Peter the Great.

GOWDY, Rev John, born 1869 in Glasgow. President, Anglo-Chinese Coll. Foochow (1904-23); Fukien Christian Univ. Foochow (1923-27). Teacher Anglo-Chinese Coll. Foochow (1928-30).

GRAHAM, Fredrick C. Campbell, born 1908 in Helensburgh. Major-General, served with distinction (1939-45) in Palestine, North Africa, Crete, Syria, India and Italy. Sometime adviser on recruiting Ministry of Defence.

GRAHAM, R.B. Cunninghame (1852-1936). Born in London, son of a Scottish Laird. Traveller, writer and politician. With Keir Hardie he organized the Scottish Labour Party. Wrote over 30 books on travel and many other stories and biographies. Was elected first President of the Scottish National Party.

GRAHAM, Ronald, born 1896 of Scottish descent. Air Vice-Marshal. Deputy senior Air Staff Officer, Fighter Command (1939), Air Officer and Air Chief of Staff H.Q. Combined Operations (1943),

A.O.C. West Africa (1944), Commandant R.A.F. Staff Coll. (1945-46), and of Scottish Police College (1949-57).

GRAHAM, Thomas (1805-69) of Glasgow. Chemist. Became first President of the Chemical Society of London. Sometime Master of the Mint.

GRAHAME, James (1765-1811) of Glasgow. Poet. Became an Advocate, then a Curate in the Church of England at Sedgefield, Durham.

GRAHAME, Kenneth (1859-1932) of Edinburgh. Author. Descendant of Robert the Bruce. Secretary to the Bank of England (1898-1907). Wrote books for children including 'The Wind in the Willows'.

GRANT, Alexander L., born 1901 in Aviemore. Appointed Director of Barclay's Bank Ltd., in 1945.

GRANT, Sir Andrew, born 1890, educ. Edinburgh. Air Marshal (1946). Director-General, R.A.F. Medical Services, Air Ministry (1946-48).

GRANT, Anne (1755-1838) of Glasgow. Poetess and Essayist. Her 'Letters from the Mountains' was a great success.

GRANT, Duncan James C., born 1885 in Rothiemurchus. Painter and designer of textiles and pottery. His painting 'Girl at the Piano' is in the Tate Gallery, London.

GRANT, Sir Francis (1803-78) of Perthshire. The leading portrait painter of his day.

GRANT, James Augustus (1827-92) of Nairn. Traveller, Explorer and writer. Was an associate of Capt. Speke on expeditions in Central Africa.

GRANT, Sir James H. (1808-75) of Kilgraston. General in the British Army. Distinguished himself in the two Sikh wars and the Indian Mutiny.

GRANT, Sir James M., born 1903, educ. Edinburgh. Lord Lyon King of Arms 1969—. Sec. to the Order of the Thistle 1971—. Writer to the Signet.

GRANT, James Macpherson (1822-85) of Alvie, Inverness-shire. Australian statesman. One of the most prominent land reformers in Australia in his day.

GRANT, John Peter (1807-93). Sometime Indian and Colonial Governor.

GRANT, John S., born 1909 in Inverness-shire. Chief Medical Officer, British Railways Bd. (1965). Medical Consultant National Freight Corp.

GRANT, Neil F., born 1882 in Forres. London editor of the Cape Times, Natal Mercury, Rand Daily Mail and Sunday Times of Johannesburg.

GRANT, Sir Patrick (1804-95) of Auchterblair. Soldier. Became a Field Marshal in 1883.

GRANT, Robert (1814-92) of Granton-on-Spey. Astronomer.

GRANT, Sir Robert McVitie (1894-1947) of Edinburgh. Sometime Chairman of McVitie & Price Ltd.

GRANT, Sir Thomas Dundas (1854-1944) of Edinburgh. Consulting Aurist and Laryngologist, London.

GRAY, Sir Alexander, born 1882 in Angus. Professor Emeritus of Political Economy, Univ. of Edinburgh, 1956—. Sat as Chairman and Member of Govt. Commissions, Committees, Courts of Inquiry, Advisory Councils etc.

GRAY, James, born 1877 in Edinburgh. Director Union Castle Mail Steamship Co. Ltd. (1950-55). Was Chief Superintending Engr., Canadian Pacific Steamships (1913-15). General Manager, and later, Director of Harland and Wolff's Works, London, Liverpool, and Southampton (1925-35).

GREEN, Cecil A., born 1908 in Dunfermline? Appointed Professor of Bacteriology, Univ. of Newcastle-upon-Tyne in 1963. Director, Dept. of Microbiology, Royal Victoria Hosp. Newcastle.

GREEN, Charles E. (1866-1920) of Edinburgh. Publisher. Founded the 'Juridical Review' (1887); 'Scots Law Times' (1891); Green's Encyclopaedia' (14 vols. 1895) and many important works on Agriculture.

GREGORY, David (1661-1708) of Kinairdy, Perthshire. Mathematician. In 1691 became Savilian Professor of Astronomy at Oxford. He first suggested an acromatic combination of lenses.

GREGORY, Sir David, born 1909 in Perthshire. Admiral Supt., H.M.

Dockyard Devonport (1960-64). Flag Officer, Scotland and N. Ireland (1964-66).

GREGORY, James (1638-75) of Drumoak, Aberdeenshire. Mathematician and Astronomer. A leading contributer to the discovery of the differential and integral calculus. Invented the reflector telescope.

GREGORY, James (1753-1821) of Aberdeen. Physician who gave his name to 'Gregorie's Mixture'.

GREIG, Alexis Samuilovich (1775-1848), son of Sir Samuel. Became an Admiral in the Russian Navy and distinguished himself in the Russo-Turkish wars (1807 and 1828-29).

GREIG, James, born 1903 in Edinburgh. Professor of Electrical Engineering, University of London, King's College 1945–.

GREIG, Sir Samuel (1735-88) of Inverness. Admiral in the Russian Navy. Fought against the Turks (1770) and the Swedes (1788).

GRIERSON, Sir Herbert J.C. (1866-1960) of Lerwick. Critic and editor. Edited the poems of Donne (1912). His studies included 'Cross Currents in the literature of the 17th century' (1929) and 'Milton and Wordsworth' (1937).

GRIERSON, Sir James M. (1859-1914) of Glasgow. Lieut.-General. Served with distinction at the battles of Kassassin and Tel-el-Kebir.

GRIERSON, John (1898-1972) of Kilmarnock. British Film Producer. General Manager Canadian wartime Information Bd. (1942-43); Director, Mass Communications UNESCO (1946-48). His productions include 'Song of Ceylon' (1934); 'Night Mail' (1936); 'World in Action' Series (1942-43) and 'This Wonderful World' (TV 1961). He was the creator of Documentary Films.

GRIEVE, Christopher Murray, (writes under the pseudonym 'Hugh McDiarmid') born 1892 in Langholm. Author, poet and journalist. Prolific writer on political and general matters. His poems include 'Three Hymns of Lenin'; 'A Kist of Whistles'; 'The Battle Continues' etc. Was a founder member of the Scottish Nationalist Party.

GRIEVE, Thomas R., born 1909, educ. Edinburgh. Chairman and Managing Director, Shell-Mex & B.P. 1965–, and of U.K. Oil Pipelines Ltd. (1965).

GRUB, George (1812-93) of Aberdeen. Church historian. Was the author of 'An Ecclesiastical History of Scotland' (1861).

GUNN, Alexander (1844-1914) of Lybster, Caithness. Surgeon. Assisted Lord Lister in his researches into the use of antiseptics.

GUNN, Sir James (1893-1965). Painter, known for his portraits of King George VI; G.K. Chesterton; Hilaire Belloc and other celebrities. Became President of the Royal Society of Portrait Painters.

GUNN, John C., born 1916 in Glasgow. Cargill Professor of Natural Philosophy. Lecturer on applied mathematics, Univ. of Manchester (1945-46) and Univ. Coll. London (1946-49).

GUNN, Neil Millar (1891-1973) of Dunbeath, Caithness. Novelist. His best known books include, 'Grey Coast'; 'Morning Tide' (1931); 'Butcher's Broom' (1934); 'Highland River' (1937); 'The Drinking Well' (1947) and 'Silver Darlings' (1951).

GUTHRIE, Sir Giles, born 1916 in Wigtownshire. Merchant Banker. Chairman, Air Transport Insurance, Lausanne, Switzerland. Director, Prudential Assurance Co., Radio Rentals Ltd. and other Companies.

GUTHRIE, Sir James (1859-1930) of Greenock. Painter. Elected R.S.A. (1892) and P.R.S.A. (1902-19).

GUTHRIE, Thomas (1803-73) of Brechin. Divine and philanthropist. In eleven months (1845-46) he raised £116,000 for providing Free Church Manses. He used his singular gifts of oratory in the causes of temperence and other social reforms, and in favour of compulsory education.

H

HADDOW, Sir Alexander, born 1907 in Broxburn. Appointed Professor of Experimental Pathology, Univ. of London in 1946. Director of Chester Beatty Research Institute, Cancer Research, Royal Cancer Hosp. Fulham Rd. (1946-69).

HADDOW, Alexander J., born 1912, educ. Glasgow. Entomologist on Yellow fever research (1942-45). Epidemiologist on East African virus research (1950-52) etc.

HAIG, Sir Douglas, 1st Earl Haig of Bemersyde (1861-1928) of Edinburgh. Field Marshal and Commander-in-Chief, British Forces in World War I.

HALDANE, Elizabeth Sanderson (1862-1937) of Edinburgh. Author.

The first woman J.P. in Scotland. Wrote 'A Life of Descartes' (1905). Translated Hagel and wrote commentaries on George Eliot (1927).

HALDANE, John Scott (1860-1936) of Edinburgh. Eminent Physiologist and authority on respiration and the effects of high and low atmospheric pressures in the organism. Made a study of the effects of industrial occupations upon physiology. Served as a Director of a mining research laboratory in Birmingham. Elected Fellow of New College, Oxford.

HALL, Basil (1788-1844) of Edinburgh. Travel writer. His works, 'Korea' (1818); 'Chile', 'Peru' and 'Mexico' (1824), and his 'Travels in North Africa' (1829) were highly popular.

HALL, Sir James (1761-1832) of Dunglass. Geologist. Sought to prove the geological theories of his friend and master (Hutton) in the laboratory, and so founded experimental geology.

HALLIDAY, Sir Andrew (1781-1839) of Dumfries. Physician. Inspector of Hospitals in West Indies (1833). Sometime physician to the Duke of Clarence.

HAMILTON, Alexander (1757-1804), born in Leeward Islands, of Scottish descent. Statesman. Private Sec. to Washington in the American War of Independence. Elected to the New York Legislature in 1787. Sec. to the Treasury (1789-95). Was killed in a duel with a political opponent.

HAMILTON, David (1768-1843) of Falkirk. Architect. His greatest work was the Palace for the Duke of Hamilton, in Lanarkshire.

HAMILTON, Douglas Douglas- (14th Duke) (1903-1973) Chief pilot, Mount Everest Flight Expedition (1933). Sometime President, Air League of the British Empire. Was premier Duke of Scotland.

HAMILTON, Iain Ellis, born 1922 in Glasgow. Composer and musician. Professor of Music, Duke Univ. North Carolina, U.S.A. His works have attracted universal interest and won the Royal Philharmonic Society prize for his Clarinet Concerto.

HAMILTON, Ian, born in Paisley? Author, journalist and drama critic. Sometime literary critic and columnist, 'Daily Telegraph'. Editorial Director, The Hutchison Group of Publishing Cos. (1958-62), Editor 'The Spectator' (1962-63). Chairman New Drama Group.

HAMILTON, James (? -d.1540) of Ayrshire. Architect of exceptional ability in his day.

HAMILTON, Tarrick (1781-1876). Linguist and Orientalist. Translator (1820) of the first four volumes of 'Sirat Anterah' (narrative of the poet Antar). Became Sec. of the British Embassy, Constantinople.

HAMILTON, William (1704-54) of Bangour. Poet, best known for his ballad 'The Braes of Yarrow'.

HAMILTON, Sir William (1788-1856) of Glasgow. Philosopher. In 1829 published, in the Edinburgh Review, a famous critique of Cousin's Doctrine of the Infinite. This and other articles were collected in 1852 as 'Discussions in Philosophy and Literature'. His principal work was his edition of Reid (1846 and 1862) defending what he believed to be Reid's philosophical doctrine of common sense, i.e. common reason.

HAMILTON, William R.D., born 1895 in Campbelltown. Major-General (1953). Consulting Physician M.E.L.F. (1948-50). Director of Medicine and Consulting Physician to the Army (1951-55).

HAMMERTON, Sir John Alexander (1871-1949) of Dumbartonshire. Editor, critic and journalist. Famous for his 'War Illustrated' of the two World Wars.

HANNAY, James (1827-73) of Dumfries. Writer. His best novels were 'Singleton Fontenoy' (1850) and 'Eustace Conyers' (1855). He was British Consul at Barcelona from 1868 until his death.

HARDIE, James Keir (1856-1915) of Legbrannock, Lanarkshire. Founder of the Independent Labour Party in 1893. In 1906 became first Chairman of the Parliamentary Labour Party.

HARDIE, Thomas (1752-1832) of Larbert. Politician. Founded in 1792 the London Corresponding Society for Parliamentary and Social Reform.

HARDIE, William F.R., born 1902 in Edinburgh. President, Corpus Christi College Oxford (1950-69).

HARRISON, James, Invented a refrigerator in 1851.

HAY, Ian, (Major-General John Hay Beith), (1876-1952), educ. Edinburgh and Cambridge. Novelist and dramatist. 'The First Hundred Thousand' (1915) and 'Carrying On' (1917) were popular books of his. Was Director of Public Relations at the War Office (1938-41).

HAY, Sir Robert, born 1889, educ. Edinburgh. Director-General, Imperial Medical Service and Hon. Physician to the King (1944-48).

HENDERSON, Arthur (1863-1935) of Glasgow. Labour politician. Home Sec. (1924); Foreign Sec. (1929-31). Was a crusader for general disarmament.

HENDERSON, Sir David (1862-1921) of Glasgow. Lieut-General. Served with distinction in Sudan and South Africa. Took up flying in 1911 and played a part in the formation of the Royal Flying Corps in 1912.

HENDERSON, David W., born 1903 in Glasgow. Director of Microbiological Research Est., Ministry of Defence 1946—.

HENDERSON, Frank Y., born 1894 in Glasgow. Director, Forest Products Research Laboratory, Dept. of Scientific and Industrial Research (1945-60).

HENDERSON, James E., born 1923, educ. Glasgow. Chief Scientist (R.A.F.) and member of the Air Force Board 1969—.

HENDERSON, Sir James T., born 1901, educ. Warriston, Moffat. Chargé d'Affaires Helsinki (1932-35); Consul-General, Houston (1949); Minister for Ireland, (1953-56) and Ambassador to Bolivia (1956-60).

HENDERSON, Dame Joan, born in Stonehaven. Director, Women's Royal Army Corps (1964-67).

HENDERSON, Joe ('Mr Piano'), born in Glasgow. Pianist, accompanist and composer.

HENDERSON, Patrick H., born 1876 in Perthshire. Major-General (1931), Served with 7th Div. in France (1914-15) with 28th Div. in Egypt and Macedonia (1916-17) and with 27th Div. in Macedonia, S. Russia, and Trans-Caspio (1917-19).

HENDERSON, Peter, born Inverness. Senior Principal Medical Officer, Ministry of Education (1964-69).

HENDERSON, Ralph, born 1897 in Perth. Director of Stores, Admiralty (1955-60).

HENDERSON, Thomas (1798-1844) of Dundee. Astronomer. In 1831 was appointed Director of the Royal Observatory at the Cape of Good Hope.

HENDRY, Arnold W., born 1921 in Buckie. Professor of Civil Engineering, Univ. of Edinburgh 1964—. University of Khartoum

(1951-57). Professor of Building Science Univ. of Liverpool (1957-63).

HENRY, Robert (1718-90) from near Stirling. Historian. Wrote the 'History of Great Britain on a new Plan' (1771-93, 6 vols.).

HERIOT, George (1563-1624) of Edinburgh. Goldsmith and philanthropist, known as 'Jingling Geordie'. Goldsmith to Anne of Denmark (1597) and later to James VI. As a court jeweller in London he amassed considerable riches. Bequeathed £23,625 to found a hospital or school in Edinburgh for "sons of poor burgesses".

HETHERINGTON, Sir Hector, born 1888 in Cowdenbeath. Principal and Vice-Chancellor Univ. of Glasgow (1936-61). Professor of Logic and Philosophy Univ. Coll. Cardiff (1915-20), Exeter (1920-24) and Liverpool (1927-36).

HIELBRON, Sir James Morris (1886-1959) of Glasgow. Organic Chemist. Professor of Organic Chemistry at Liverpool (1920), Manchester (1933) and at Imperial Coll. London (1938-49), was best known for his work on vitimins A and D. Elected F.R.S. in 1931.

HIGHET, Gilbert, born 1906 in Glasgow. Scholar, critic and author. Appointed Professor of Greek and Latin in Columbia Univ. in 1938. Wrote 'Man's Unconquerable Mind'.

HILL, David Octavius (1802-70). Landscape and portrait painter. First to apply photography to portraiture.

HILL, Ian G.W., born 1904 in Edinburgh. Professor of Medicine Univ. of St Andrews 1950—. Consulting Physician, 14th Army Burma and A.L.F.S.E.A. (1944-45). Patel Lecturer, Bombay (1961).

HOARE, Sir Samuel, born 1896 in Inverness. Asst. Under-Sec. of State, Home Office (1946-61). Represented the U.K. on various international bodies, including Narcotics Commission and Economic and Social Council of U.N.

HOGG, James (1770-1835) of Ettrick, Stirlingshire. Poet of force and originality. 'The Queen's Wake' (1813) was one of his best.

HOLDEN, Sir Isaac (1807-97) of Hurlet, Renfrewshire. Inventor. Studied chemistry in his leisure hours. Invented the 'Lucifer' match, but was anticipated by John Walker of Stockton.

HOLMES, William, born 1922 in Kilbarchan, Renfrewshire. Professor of Agriculture, Wye Coll. Univ. London 1955—. President, British

Society of Animal Production (1969-70). Sometime Adviser to Tech. Committee, Univ. of West Indies.

HONEYMAN, Alexander M., born 1907 in Fife? Professor of Oriental languages, Univ. of St Andrews 1936–. External examiner to Univs. of Glasgow, Edinburgh, Belfast, Leeds and London. Travelled and excavated in S. Arabia 1950-54 and 58.

HONEYMAN, Sir George, born 1898 in Glasgow. Chairman, Civil Service Arbitration Tribunal (1952), Agricultural Wages Bd. (1953); Comm. of Inquiry, Copper Mining Industry, N. Rhodesia (1957); Board of Inquiry, Sugar Milling Industry, Fiji (1959), etc.

HOOD, Sir Alexander, born 1888 in Edinburgh. Lieut-General (1941). Sometime Deputy Director of Medical Services, British Forces in Palestine and Trans-Jordan. Director-General Army Medical Services (1941-48). Governor and C-in-C, Bermuda (1949-55).

HOPE, John A. Louis (7th Earl and 1st Marquis of Linlithgow), (1860-1908). Appointed first Governor-General of Australia (1900-02).

HOPE, Thomas Charles (1766-1844) of Edinburgh. Chemist and lecturer. Carried out important researches in physics. Conclusively confirmed the 17th century observation, in his day regarded with scepticism — that water expands as it nears freezing.

HOPE, Victor Alexander John (8th Earl and 2nd. Marquis of Linlithgow), (1887-1952). Viceroy of India (1936-43).

HORNE, Henry Sinclair, 1st. Baron of Stirkok. Commanded 1st Army in France (1916). General Officer Commanding-in-Chief, Eastern Command (1919-23). Was first to use the 'Creeping Barrage' system of artillary support for infantry.

HOUSTON, Renée (Katherina Houston Gribbin). Vaudeville and Review artist. Once teamed with her sister Billie. More recently, character artist on Screen and TV. A very popular member of radio's 'Petticoat Line' team.

HOWSON, John, born 1908 in Glasgow? Rear Admiral (1961). Served with distinction in H.M.S. Newcastle and H.M.S. Nelson (1939-44). Chief of Staff to C-in-C Plymouth (1958-61). Commander, Allied Naval Forces, Northern Europe (1961-62). Regional Officer, N. Midlands, British Productivity Council 1964–.

HOYER-MILLAR, Dame Elizabeth, born in Angus. Director, Women's

Royal Naval Service (1958-61). Hon. A.D.C. to the Queen (1958-61).

HUGHES, Henry H., born 1911 Educ. Clydebank and Glasgow. Rear Admiral (1964). Director of Naval Electrical Engineering 1964—.

HUME, Joseph (1777-1855) of Montrose. Radical politician. Sat in Parliament (1812 and 1819-55). Advocated savings banks, freedom of trade with India, abolition of flogging in the army, of naval impressment and of imprisonment for debt, and repeal of the act prohibiting export of machinery, and of that preventing workmen from going abroad.

HUMPHREYS, Eliza M. (died 1938) from near Inverness. Novelist who wrote under the pen-name 'Rita'. Of some 60 novels, 'Souls' (1903) was the one that made her famous. In the days of Victorian conventions, she was reckoned a daring novelist.

HUNTER, John (1728-93) of Long Calderwood, E.Kilbride. Physiologist and Surgeon. Founder of scientific surgery. In 1776 was appointed surgeon extraordinary to the King. His 'Natural History of Human Teeth' (1771-78) revolutionised dentistry.

HUNTER, William (1718-83) of Long Calderwood. Anatomist and Obstetrician. In 1764 appointed Physician extraordinary to Queen Charlotte. His chief work was on the uterus. Elected F.R.S. in 1767.

HUNTER, Sir William Wilson (1840-1900) of Glasgow. Statistician. Director-General of the Statistical Dept. of India (1871). The Indian census of 1872 was his work.

HUTCHISON, Sir Balfour O., born 1889 in Kirkcaldy. Lieut-General. Deputy Q.M.G. Middle East (1940-42); G.O.C. Sudan and Eritrea (1942-43); Q.M.G. India (1944-45) (Ret.) Served with distinction in Palestine Rebellion (1938-39).

HUTCHISON, James H., born 1912 in Glasgow. Samson Gemmel Professor of Child Health. Produced many publications on Paediatric problems, rickets and genetic diseases in childhood.

HUTCHISON, James S., born 1904 in Glasgow. Chairman British Oxygen Co. Ltd. and associated Companies 1950—.

HUTCHISON, Sir William Oliphant, born 1889 in Fife. Portrait painter. President, Royal Society of Portrait Painters (1965). His sitters included H.M. The Queen and H.R.H. Prince Philip Duke of Edinburgh.

HUTTON, James (1726-97) of Edinburgh. Geologist. The 'Huttonian' theory, emphasizing the igneous origin of many rocks and deprecating the assumption of other causes than those we see still at work, was expounded before the Royal Society of Edinburgh in 'A Theory of the Earth' (1785). It formed the basis of modern geology.

I

IMRIE, Sir John D., born 1891 in Kinross? Educ. Edinburgh. Chartered Accountant. Local Govt. Commissioner, West Indies (1951-53). Director Caledonian Ins. Co. Ltd.

INCHCAPE, (Kenneth J.W. Mackay) 3rd Earl, born 1917. Director P. & O. Steam Navigation Co.; The Chartered Bank; Royal Exchange Assurance; Burma Oil Co.; B.P. Co.; Commonwealth Development Finance Co. etc. Appointed Chairman P. & O. in 1973.

INNES, Cosmo (1798-1874) of Deeside. Antiquary, historian and editor. Author of 'Scotland in the Middle Ages' (1860) and 'Sketches of Early Scottish History' (1861).

INNES, Lewis (1651-1738) of Banffshire. Became Principal of the Scots College Paris.

INNES, Thomas (1662-1744) of Aboyne, Aberdeenshire. Historian and Antiquary. Became vice-Principal of Scots Coll. Paris. Wrote 'Critical Essay on the Ancient Inhabitants of the Northern Parts of Britain' (1729).

INNES, Sir Thomas of Learney, born 1893. Lord Lyon King of Arms and Sec. to the Order of the Thistle (1946-69). Published many articles on Scots Heraldry, History and Peerage Law.

INVERCLYDE, (Sir John Burns) 1st Baron (1829-1901) of Glasgow. Brother of Sir George, Chairman of the Cunard Steamship Co.

INVERCLYDE, (Sir George A. Burns) 2nd Baron (1861-1905) of Glasgow. Followed his brother John as Chairman of the Cunard Steamship Co.

INVERFORTH, (Sir Andrew A.M. Weir) 2nd Baron, born 1897. Chairman and Governing Director of Andrew Weir & Co. Ltd.

IRONSIDE, William E., 1st Baron (1880-1959) of Aberdeenshire. Soldier. Chief of Imperial General Staff at outbreak of World War II.

Promoted Field Marshal (1940) in charge of Home Defence Forces.

IRVINE, James Colquhoun (1877-1952) of Glasgow. Chemist. Famous for researches in carbohydrate chemistry.

IRVING, David (1778-1860) of Langholm. Biographer. Librarian and editor. In 1820 was appointed Principal Librarian of the Faculty of Advocates.

IRVING, David B., born 1903 in Ayrshire. Chairman London Electricity Board (1956-58); British Electricity Development Assoc. (1960-61) and Power Division I.E.E. (1962-63).

IRVING, Edward (1792-1834) of Annan. Divine, who, from 1822 till his death was one of the most notable preachers in London (Scotch Church in Hatton Garden and a new church in Regent Sq). A man of striking appearance and fine voice.

IRVING, John, born 1920 in Hamilton? Professor of Natural Philosophy. Senior lecturer in applied mathematics, Univ. of Southampton (1951-59). Professor and head of Dept. of Applied Mathematics and Theoretical Physics, Univ. of Cape Town (1959-61).

IRVING, Washington (1783-1859), born in New York, son of a Scottish emigrant. Essayist and historian. 'The Sketch Book' (1819) which contained 'Rip Van Winkle' and 'The Legend of Sleepy Hollow' was a great success. His crowning work was the 'Life of Washington' (1855-59).

ISAACS, Alick (1921-67) of Glasgow. Virologist and discoverer of Interferon.

IVORY, James (1765-1842) A brilliant Scottish mathematician who won considerable fame in his day.

J

JACK, Sir Daniel, born 1901 in Glasgow. Professor of Economics Univ. of Durham and King's Coll. Newcastle-upon-Tyne (1950-55). Chairman Court of Inquiry, Shipping and Engineering wages dispute (1957); London Airport dispute (1958) and Ford dispute (1963). Appointed Chairman, Air Transport Board in 1961.

JACK, Gilbert (c. 1578-1628) of Aberdeen. Metaphysician and medical writer. Was first to teach metaphysics at Leyden. Declined a professorship at Oxford in 1621.

JACK, Robert L., born 1845 in Irvine. Consulting Geologist, Mining engineer and explorer in Queensland. Was Govt. Geologist for Queensland (1877-99).

JACK, William (1795-1822) of Aberdeen. Botanist and Surgeon. Appointed Surgeon in Bengal Medical Service when aged 18.

JACK, William (1834-1924) of Stewarton. Astronomer and Philosopher. Professor of Astronomy Univ. of Glasgow and Prof. of Natural Philosophy, Manchester (1866-70).

JACKSON, Gordon, born 1923 in Glasgow. Appeared in many films incl. 'The Captive Heart' (1946); 'Whisky Galore' (1948); 'The Lady with a Lamp' (1951); 'Tunes of Glory' (1960); 'Cast a Giant Shadow' (1966). Popular as the butler in TVs 'Upstairs Downstairs' 1972—.

JACOB, Violet, (Kennedy-Erskine) (1863-1946) of Montrose. Poetess and novelist. Her poems incl. 'The Northern Lights' (1927), and two of her best known novels are 'The Interloper' (1904) and 'Flemington' (1911).

JAMESON, George (1588-1644) of Aberdeen. Portrait painter.

JARDINE PATERSON, Sir John, born in Lockerbie. President Bengal Chamber of Commerce and Industry (1966) and Assoc. Chamber of Commerce, India. Member of local board Reserve Bank of India (1965-67) and many other important posts at home and abroad.

JARVIE, John G., born 1883 in Carluke. Founder and Chairman from its beginning in 1919 of United Dominions Trust Ltd. and the U.D.T. Group of Companies until 1963 when he retired from the Chair and became President.

JOHNSTON, Alexander Keith (1844-79) of Edinburgh. Writer of Geographical works. In 1879 was appointed leader of the Royal Geographical Society's expedition to East Africa.

JOHNSTON or RONSTON, Arthur (1587-1641) of Aberdeenshire. Physician and Humanist. Practised medicine in France whence his fame as a Latin poet spread over Europe. About 1625 he was appointed Physician to King Charles I.

JOHNSTONE, Alan S., born in Dumfriesshire. Professor of Radio-diagnosis, Univ. of Leeds (1948-68). President, Thoracic Society of Gt. Britain (1961-62). Produced several publications on Radiology.

JOHNSTONE, Alexander V.R., born 1916 in Glasgow. Air Vice-Marshal founder of Malayan Air Force (1957); Director of personnel Air Ministry (1962-64); A.O.C. No. 18 Gp. and Maritime Air Commander, North Atlantic, N.A.T.O. (1965-68).

JORDAN, Sydney, born 1929? in Dundee. Author and cartoonist. Creater of 'Jeff Hawke' the Daily Express cartoon spaceman. Awarded the Prix St Michel by a European Cartoonists Assoc. in 1973.

JUNOR, John, born 1919 in Black Isle. Editor, Sunday Express 1954—. Director, Sunday Express 1957—. Director of Beaverbrook Newspapers 1960—. Was Deputy editor, Evening Standard (1953-54).

JUSTICE, James Robertson, born 1905. Actor and Personality, and former journalist and naturalist. Starred in many American and British films, incl. 'Scott of the Antarctic' (1948); 'Whisky Galore' (1949); 'Doctor in the House' (1954); 'Campbell's Kingdom' (1957); 'Doctor at Large' (1958); 'Chitty Chitty Bang Bang' (1968).

K

KAY, Sir James R., born 1885 in Glasgow. President, Imperial Bank of India (Bengal), (1933-34; 35-36 and 39-40). Pres. Associated Chambers of Commerce of India (1937-38).

KAY, Katharine Cameron, born Glasgow. Painter and Etcher. Exhibited at the Royal Academy, Royal Scottish Academy, Berlin, Liverpool, Venice, Leipzig etc.

KEILLER, Mrs Keiller of Dundee. Invented marmalade in 1797. Her son founded the Keiller Co., and marmalade became popular throughout the world.

KEIR, Andrew, born 1926 in Shotts. Actor. Popular as 'Adam Smith' the Scottish minister on TV. Played 'Cromwell' in 'A Man for all Seasons', Prince John in TVs 'Ivanhoe'. Won an award for his leading part in 'Soldier Soldier'.

KEIR, James (1735-1820) of Edinburgh. Pioneer of industrial chemistry.

KEITH, Sir Arthur (1866-1955) from Persley near Aberdeen. Anatomist and Anthropologist. Wrote 'Introduction to the Study of Anthropoid Apes' (1896); 'Human Embryology and Morphology' (1901), and works on ancient man. Elected F.R.S.

KEITH, George (1685-1778). Close friend of Frederick the Great. He was the last Earl Marshal of Scotland.

KEITH, James (1696-1758) of Inverugie, near Peterhead. Was Commander-in-Chief to Frederick the Great in the Prussian Army.

KELLAS, Arthur R.H., born 1915, educ. Aberdeen and Oxford. Counsellor H.M. Embassy and Consul-General, Tel-Aviv 1964—.

KELVIN OF LARGS. (William Thomson) 1st Baron (1824-1907) born in Belfast of Scottish descent. Physicist, Mathematician, Philosopher and engineer. Discovered the second law of thermodynamics. Inventor of telegraphic and scientific instruments etc. incl. the improved mariners compass and sounding equipment. Elected F.R.S. in 1851. Buried in Westminster Abbey.

KEMP, George Meikle (1795-1844) from near Biggar. Draughtsman and Architect. Designer of the Scott Monument Edinburgh.

KENNEDY, David (? -d.1886) of Perth. Singer who had great success in London, Australia, South Africa, New Zealand, India, Canada, and the U.S.A.

KENNEDY, Sir James Shaw (1788-1865) of Kirkcudbrightshire. Soldier. Became a General and distinguished himself under Wellington.

KENNEDY, John (1769-1855) of Kirkcudbrightshire. Cottonspinner and inventor. Introduced several ingenious improvements in the spinning of fine yarns, including the 'Jack frame'.

KENNEDY, Ludovic H.C., born 1919 in Edinburgh. Writer, Film director and broadcaster.

KER, William Paton (1855-1923) of Glasgow. Scholar, Talker, Lecturer and Writer. Professor of English at Cardiff (1883); at London (1889) and of poetry at Oxford (1920). He died of heart failure while climbing in the Alps at the age of 67.

KERR, John (1824-1907) of Ardrossan. Physicist and lecturer in mathematics. In 1876 he discovered the 'magneto-optic effect' which was then named after him. He was the author of 'An Elementary Treatise on Rational Mechanics' (1867). Elected F.R.S.

KIDD, Margaret H. (Mrs Margaret Macdonald), educ. Linlithgow. Sheriff Principal of Perth and Angus 1966—. (Of Dumfries and

Galloway 1960-66).

KIDSON, William, born 1849 in Falkirk. Became Prime Minister of Australia in 1906.

KILBRANDON, (Charles J.D. Shaw) Baron (life peer) of Kilbrandon, Argyll, born 1906. Lord of Appeal in Ordinary 1971—. Member, Commission on the Constitution 1969—.

KILMARNOCK, (Gilbert A.R. Boyd) 6th Baron, born 1903, son of the 21st Earl of Errol. Chairman, Baltic and Mercantile Shipping Exchange (1965-67). Was President, London Chamber of Commerce (1961-63). Freeman of the City of London.

KILMUIR, Viscount, formerly, Sir David P. Maxwell-Fyfe, born 1900 in Aberdeen? Lawyer and politician. Was Deputy Chief Prosecuter at the Nuremberg Trial of Nazi war criminals.

KING, Alexander, born 1909 in Glasgow. Director-General for Scientific Affairs O.E.C.D. 1961—.

KINNAIRD, Arthur F., 10th Baron (1814-87) of Perthshire. Banker and philanthropist.

KINROSS, (John P.D. Balfour) 3rd Baron of Glasclune, born 1904. Author and journalist. Travelled extensively in the Middle East, Africa and elsewhere. Was first Sec. and Director, Publicity Section, British Embassy Cairo (1944-47).

KIRK, James B., born 1893 in Falkirk. Director Medical and Health Dept., Mauritious (1926-41), of Medical Services, Gold Coast (1941-44) of Health Div. Greece Mission UNRRA, (1945). Chief Medical Officer, Central H.Q. Displaced Persons Operations, UNRRA, Germany (1945).

KIRKPATRICK, Charles (1879-1955) of Pitlochry. Major-General (1929) in the Indian Army. Served with distinction in World War I and on the N.W. Frontier.

KIRKPATRICK, Herbert James, born 1910, son of Major-General Charles. Air Vice Marshal, served on Air Staff, Fighter Commd. (1939-40); Bomber Commd. (1941-45), and Transport Commd. (1946-48). Chief of Staff 2nd Allied Tactical Air Force (1957-60). A.O.C. No. 25 Group (1961-63).

KNOX, Henry M., born 1916 in Edinburgh. Professor of Education at Queen's Univ. Belfast 1951—.

KNOX, John (1505-72) of Haddington. Preacher and Reformationist. Founder of the Presbyterian Church.

KNOX, John, born 1913, educ. in Glasgow. Scientist. Appointed Chief Scientific Officer, Min. of Technology in 1965. Head of Research Div. Dept. of Trade and Industry 1971—.

KNOX, Joseph A.C., born 1911 in Aberdeen. Professor of Physiology, Univ. of London at Queen Elizabeth Coll., 1954—.

KNOX, Robert (1791-1862) of Edinburgh. Anatomist. Attracted considerable odium through having obtained subjects for dissection from Burke and Hare.

KYLE, Elizabeth (Agnes M.R. Dunlop) of Ayrshire. Novelist and writer of books for children. Since her first novel in 1932 she published over 50 books.

L

LAING, Alexander Gordon (1793-1826) of Edinburgh. Explorer. Served as an officer in the West Indies for 7 years. Was sent to explore the Niger's source, which he found, but was murdered after leaving Timbuktu.

LAING, David (1793-1878) of Edinburgh. Antiquary. From 1837 was Librarian to the Signet Library.

LAING, Malcolm (1762-1818) of Orkney. Historian. He it was who completed Henry's 'History of Great Britain' (1793) and in 1802 published his own 'History of Scotland (1603-1701)'.

LAING, Samuel (1780-1868) of Orkney. Travelled and wrote in Norway, Sweden, Russia, France etc.

LAING, W.J. Scott, born 1914, educ. Edinburgh. Chief, Sales Section U.N. Secretariat 1969—. Was Consul, New York (1950) and Consul-General (Commercial) New York (1954).

LAIRD, John (1805-74) of Greenock. Shipbuilder. One of the earliest constructors of iron vessels.

LAIRD, John (1887-1946) of Kincardineshire. Philosopher. Professor at Dalhousie, Nova Scotia (1912); Belfast (1913-24) and Aberdeen (1924-26).

LAMOND, Fredric (1868-1948) of Glasgow. Pianist and composer. Made his début at Berlin in 1885. He excelled in playing Beethoven.

LAMONT, Johann von (1805-79) of Braemar, Aberdeenshire. Astronomer. Appointed Director of Bogenhausen Observatory in 1835, and in 1852 became Professor of Astronomy at Munich.

LANG, Andrew (1844-1912) of Selkirk. Scholar and writer of poetry, fiction, fairy tales, folklore and translations from classics. Published a 'History of Scotland' (1900-07).

LANG, Cosmo G., Baron Lang of Lambeth (1864-1945) of Fyvie. Anglican Prelate. Appointed Archbishop of York in 1928 and Archbishop of Canterbury in 1942.

LAPWORTH, Arthur (1892-1941) of Galashiels. Organic chemist. Remembered for his enunciation of the electronic theory of organic clinical reactions in 1920. Appointed to the Chair of Physical and Inorganic Chemistry in 1922. Elected F.R.S.

LAUDER, Sir Harry Maclennan (1870-1950) of Portobello. Comedian, singer and composer. 'Roamin in the Gloamin'; 'Tobermory'; 'A Wee Deoch and Doris'; 'The Lass of Killiecrankie'; 'I Love a Lassie' are some of his best remembered.

LAUDER, Sir Thomas Dick (1784-1848) of Haddington. Novelist and journalist. Best known for 'The Wolf of Badenoch' (1827) and his 'Account of the Great Floods in Morayshire' (1829).

LAURIE, John, born 1897. Character actor on stage and screen. Popular member of 'Dad's Army' series on TV.

LAURIE, Sir John E., born 1892. Major-General. Commanded the 6th Bn. Seaforth Hrs. (1918-19), and 2nd Seaforth Hrs. (1934-38) the Tientsin Area British Troops in China (1939-40); No. 157 Infantry Bde., France (1940) and 52nd Lowland Div. (1941-42).

LAURIE, Sir Peter (1778-1861) of Haddington. Son of a farmer, became Lord Mayor of London in 1832.

LAW, A. Bonar (1858-1923) of Glasgow? Prime Minister of Britain (1922-23).

LAW, John (1671-1729) of Edinburgh. Financier. Founder of the first Bank of France, having failed in Britain to introduce paper currency.

LEASK, Sir Henry, born 1913. Lieut-General. G.O.C. Scotland and

Governor of Edinburgh Castle 1969—.

LEASK, Kenneth, born 1896 in Birsay, Orkney. Air Vice Marshal. Senior Engineering Staff Officer, H.Q. R.A.F. India (1933-34) and H.Q. A.D.G.B. Bomber Commd. (1934-40). Director-General of Engineering, Air Ministry (1947-49).

LECKIE, Robert, educ. Glasgow. Air Marshal. Director of Flying Operations, Canadian Air Board (1920); Commander (RAF) on H.M.S. Hermes and Courageous (Aircraft carriers) (1925-29). Director of Training, Air Ministry (1935-38) and Chief of Staff R.C.A.F. (1944).

LEE, James Paris (1831-1904) of Hawick. Watchmaker. Invented the remarkably efficient bolt action and magazine of the Lee-Metford (later Lee-Enfield) rifle about 1890.

LEE, Robert (1804-68) of Tweedsmouth. Divine and Reformationist. His introduction of a harmonica (1863) and an organ (1865) and standing during the singing of hymns, brought bitter attacks upon him.

LEGGE, James (1815-97) of Huntly. Chinese scholar. Took charge of the Anglo-Chinese College in Malacca, then laboured 30 years at Hong Kong. In 1876 became Professor of Chinese at Oxford.

LEISHMAN, Sir William B. (1896-1926) of Glasgow. Bacteriologist. Professor of Pathology in the Army Medical Coll. and Director-General Army Medical Service (1923). He discovered an effective vaccine for innoculation against typhoid, and was first to discover the parasite of the disease kala-azar.

LEITCH, Isabella, of Peterhead. Director, Commonwealth bureau of Animal Nutrition (1940-60). Produced several publications on Genetics, Physiology and Nutrition.

LEITCH, William Leighton (1804-83) of Glasgow. Water-colour painter. Was drawing master to Queen Victoria and the Royal Family for 22 years.

LEITH, Sir James (1763-1816) of Aberdeenshire. Lieut-General. Distinguished himself at Corunna, Busaco, Badajoz and Salamanca.

LENNON, Gordon, born 1911 in Aberdeen. Dean of the Faculty of Medicine Univ. of Australia, Perth, (1967). Visiting Professor Iraq, Turkey, South Africa and Uganda (1958) and Iran (1959).

LESLIE, Alexander, 1st Earl of Leven (1580-1661) of Cupar-Angus. General. Won much distinction in 30 years in the armies of Charles II and Gustavus Adolphus of Sweden. He also distinguished himself at Marston Moor for Charles I. Returned to Scotland in 1638 to serve with the Covenanters.

LESLIE, David (? -d.1682) of Fifeshire. General. Served with distinction with Gustavus Adolphus of Sweden. Returned to Scotland about 1643 to aid the Covenanters.

LESLIE or LESLEY, John (1527-96), son of the Rector of Kingussie. Was the confidential friend of Mary Queen of Scots, who made him her Ambassador to Queen Elizabeth of England. He became Vicar-General of the diocese of Rouen in 1579.

LESLIE, Sir John (1766-1832) of Largo, Fifeshire. Mathematician and Natural Philosopher. Travelled as a tutor in America and in the Continent. Invented a Differential Thermometer, Hygrometer, Photometer, Pyrometer, Atometer and Althriscope. His researches appeared in 1804 in his 'Experimental Inquiry into the Nature and Properties of Heat'. In 1810 he successfully applied the absorbent powers of sulphuric acid to freeze water under the receiver of the airpump. This is the first recorded achievement of artificial congelation.

LESLIE, Walter (1606-67). General and Diplomat. Served with distinction in Germany against the Swedes.

LEYDEN, John (1775-1811) of Denholm, Roxburghshire. Poet and Orientalist. Studied medicine, was licensed as a preacher in 1798. Sailed to India (1803) as Asst. Surgeon at Madras. Travelled widely in the east. Acquired 34 languages and translated the Gospels into five of them.

LIND, James (1716-94) of Edinburgh. Physician. His work towards the cure and prevention of scurvy, induced the Admiralty in 1795 to issue the order that the Navy should be supplied with lemon juice. His 'A Treatise of Scurvy' (1753) was, and is, a classic of medical literature, and won him an international reputation.

LINDSAY, Alexander Dunlop. 1st Baron Lindsay of Birker (1879-1952) of Glasgow. Scholar and lecturer. In 1949 was appointed head of the new Univ. Coll. of North Staffordshire. Vice-Chancellor of Oxford (1935-38).

LINDSAY, Edward S., born 1905 in Fife. Major-General (Ret.) Controller of Munitions, Min. of Supply (1961), (Deputy Controller 1957-61). Principal Staff Officer to High Commissioner, Malaya

(1954-56).

LINKLATER, Eric, born 1899 in Dounby, Orkney. Novelist and playwright. Was for a time after World War I, a journalist in Bombay. A prolific writer. His filmed works include; 'Poet's Pub', 'Private Angelo' and 'Laxdale Hall'. Was awarded the Carnegie medal for 'The Wind on the Moon'.

LIPTON, Sir Thomas Johnstone, (1850-1931) of Glasgow. Business man, Philanthropist, Tea trader, Chain store operator and Yacht racer.

LISTON, Robert (1794-1847) of Linlithgow. Surgeon, whose skill won him a European reputation. In 1835 he became Professor of Clinical Surgery at the Univ. Coll. London. He was the first to use a general anaesthetic in a public operation (1846). In the pre-anaesthetic era he amputated a patient's leg, through the thigh in 33 seconds, and accidentally cut three fingers off his assistant in the process. Is said to have been a man of herculean strength.

LITHGOW, William (1582-1645?) of Lanark. Traveller. In 1612 set out on foot from Paris to Palestine and Egypt. His Second tramp (1614-16) led him through North Africa from Tunis to Fez and home by way of Hungary and Poland. In his last journey (1619-21) to Spain via Ireland he was seized as a spy at Malaga and tortured. He claimed to have tramped 36,000 miles in 19 years.

LIVINGSTONE, David (1813-73) of Blantyre. Explorer and missionary in Africa. Discovered the Zambezi river, Victoria falls, lakes Nyasa, Shirwa, Mweru and Bangweulu. Buried in Westminster Abbey.

LOCKHART, John Gibson (1794-1854) of Lanarkshire. Biographer and novelist. His 'Life of Scott' (1838) is regarded as one of the greatest biographies in the language.

LOCKHART, Sir Robert H. Bruce, born 1887 in Anstruther. Author and journalist. Between 1911 and 1917 was British Vice-Consul then Consul in Moscow. His books include 'Memoirs of a British Agent', 'Retreat from Glory', 'Comes the Reckoning' and 'My Europe'.

LOCKHART, William Ewert (1846-1900) of Annan. Subject painter. Painted the Jubilee celebrations in Westminster (1887). Was popular too as a portrait-painter. Elected F.R.S. in 1878.

LOGAN, Jimmy, born 1928 in Glasgow. Actor/Comedian. Appeared in many TV variety shows including his own TV Series (1959-61).

London Palladium (1969-70). etc.

LORIMER, James (1818-90) of Perthshire. Jurist and writer. Was an eminent authority on International Law. 'The Institutes of the Law of Nations' was his best selling book.

LORIMER, Sir Robert Stodart (1864-1929) of Perthshire. Architect. The architect of the Scottish War Memorial at Edinburgh Castle and the Thistle Chapel in St. Giles, which brought him international recognition.

LOUDON, John C., (1783-1843) of Cambuslang. Horticulturist. Studied landscape gardening, working in England and travelling in Europe. The results of his studies are to be found in his many works, including his 'Encyclopaedia of Gardening' (1822).

LOW, Sir Francis, born 1893 in Aberdeenshire. Editor of the 'Evening News' of India (1922); news editor 'Times of India' (1925) and Editor (1932-48). President of Bombay Y.M.C.A. (1943-48).

LOVAT, (Simon C.J. Fraser) 17th Baron, born 1911. Distinguished himself as a Brigadier in the Commandos in 1943. Under Sec. of State for Foreign Affairs 1945—.

LUCAS, Raleigh B., born 1914 in Edinburgh. Professor of Oral Pathology, Univ. of London 1954—. Consultant Pathologist, Royal Dental Hosp. of London 1950—.

LULU, (Marie Lawrie) of Glasgow. Actress and singer. Had her own, very successful TV series with the B.B.C. Is very popular in America.

LYALL, William C., born 1921, educ. Kelty. Consul-General, Genoa 1969—.

LYELL, Sir Charles (1797-1875) of Kinnordy, near Kirriemuir. Geologist. His 'Principals of Geology' (1830-33) may be ranked with Darwin's 'Origin of Species', among the books which exercised the most powerful influence on scientific thought in the 19th century. It denied the necessity of stupendous convulsions and taught that the greatest geological changes may have been produced by forces still at work. Buried in Westminster Abbey.

LYNEDOCH, Thomas Graham, 1st Baron (1748-1843) of Balgowan. Raised in 1793 the 99th Regiment of Foot and served at Quiberon and in Minorca (1798); besieged Valetta (1800); was at Corruna and Walcheren (1807); defeated the French at Barrosa (1811); Captured Tolosa (1813) and Sebastian, and in Holland conquered at Marxem.

LYNDSAY or LINDSAY, Sir David (c. 1486-1555) of, probably near Coupar. Poet and satirist. Went on Embassies to the Netherlands, France, England and Denmark. His poems, often coarse, are full of humour and knowledge of the world and were said to have done more for the Reformation in Scotland than all the sermons of Knox.

M

(ALL names beginning Mc or Mac are treated as if they began Mac.)

MacADAM, Sir Ivison, born 1894 in Edinburgh. Editor of 'The Annual Register of World Events'.

MacADAM, John Loudon (1756-1836) of Ayr. Inventor of the Macadamizing system of road-making, commonly known as 'Tarmac'. Appointed surveyor of Britain's roads in 1827. He refused a Knighthood.

McALISTER, Arthur, born 1818 of Glasgow. Prime Minister of Australia in 1866.

McALPINE, Sir Robert, of Newarthill near Glasgow. Founder of the Sir Robert McAlpine Construction and Property Empire. Pioneered the widespread uses of concrete in Britain.

McARTHUR, Helen, of Glasgow. Singer. Became popular in radio's 'Friday Night is Music Night'. Gained 'Top female radio personalty' award of 1971. Had her own TV series 'The Helen McArthur Show'.

MacARTHUR, John (1767-1834). Known as the Father of New South Wales. Introduced sheep and planted the first vineyard in Australia in 1817.

MacARTHUR, Wilson, born 1903 in Ayr? Author, freelance journalist and broadcaster.

MacAULAY, Thomas B. Lord (1800-59). Brilliant historian. Sometime Secretary for War and Paymaster-General. Wrote a 'History of England'.

MacBAIN, Sir James (1828-92) of Ross-shire. Brilliant statesman, became a cabinet minister and was Director of two Banks and three Insurance Offices.

MacCALL, Charles J., born 1907 in Edinburgh. Artist. Painter of portraits, landscapes and contemporary life. Exhibited regularly in

London. One-man shows in Leicester, Dublin, New York, Manchester, Montreal and London.

McCALL, Frederick, of Glasgow. Sometime Director of Veterinary Services, Tanganyika. (retired).

McCALL, Sir Henry W.U., born 1895 in Ayrshire? Admiral (1953). Naval Attaché, Buenos Aires (1938-40); Senior British Naval Officer, Middle East (1946-48); Flag Officer Destroyers, Mediterranean Fleet (1949-50) and other Naval appointments.

McCALL, Robert C., born 1906 in Glasgow. Controller of Northern Ireland B.B.C. (1956-66).

McCLINTOCK, Sir Francis L. (1819-1907). Admiral and Polar explorer. Was knighted for discovering the fate of the Franklin expedition.

MacCOLL, Dugald Sutherland (1859-1948) of Glasgow. Painter, poet and art historian. Keeper of the Tate Gallery (1906-11) and of the Wallace Collection (1911-24).

McCRAE, John (1872-1918), born in Ontario of Scottish parents. Doctor and poet. When a Medical Officer in the first World War, wrote 'Flanders Fields', one of the great war poems which appeared in 1915.

MacCULLOCH, Sir James, born 1819 in Glasgow. Prime Minister of Australia in 1863.

McCULLOCH, John Ramsay (1789-1864) of Whithorn. Political economist. In 1828 became Professor of Political Economy Univ. Coll. London, and Comptroller of H.M. Stationery Office in 1838.

MacCUMM, Hamish (1868-1916) of Greenock. Musical composer and song writer of remarkable individuality.

McDONALD, Alexander, born 1903, educ. Edinburgh. Secretary of the Institute of Civil Engineers 1954—. Director of Public Works, Sierra Leone (1942-43). Inspector-General of Public Works, Nigeria, (1951 -54).

MacDONALD, Angus Alexr., born 1904, educ. Edinburgh. Deputy Commissioner, Lyallpur (1933-36); Amritsar (1936-41); Deputy Home Sec. Punjab (1941-43) and Home Sec. Punjab (1943-47), (retired).

MacDONALD, Sir Claud (1852-1915). Sometime British Minister at Peking.

MacDONALD, Donald M.T., born 1909 in Isle of Skye. Air Vice Marshal, Director-General of Manning, Air Ministry (1956-61) (retired).

MacDONALD, Flora (1722-90) of South Uist. Conducted Prince Charles Edward Stewart to safety in Skye in 1746, disguised as 'Betty Burke'.

MacDONALD, George (1824-1905) of Huntly. Poet and novelist. 'David Elginbrod' (1862); 'The Marquis of Lossie' (1877) and 'Sir Gibbie' (1879) are three of his best novels.

MacDONALD, Harry, born 1886 in Isle of Skye. Major-General (1940), General Staff Officer, Western Commd. India (1928-31). Major-General, Cavalry, India (1939-40), and other high appointments in India.

MacDONALD, Sir Hector (1853-1903) of Dingwall. Soldier, who rose from the ranks and became a General. Alleged to have been involved in the Russo-Japanese war. Distinguished himself at Omdurman.

MacDONALD, Iverach, born 1908, son of Benjamin MacDonald of Strathcool, Caithness. Associate editor of 'The Times' newspaper (1967-68), and Director 1968—.

MacDONALD, James Ramsay (1866-1937) of Lossiemouth. First Labour Prime Minister of Britain in 1924 (Jan. to Nov.). Re-elected Prime Minister in 1929 and formed a National Government in 1931 during the financial crisis.

McDONALD, Sir John, born 1898, son of Donald McDonald of Falkirk. Minister for Water Supply and Electricity, in Victoria, Australia (1943-45); Minister for Lands etc. (1947-48) and Premier and Treasurer, Victoria, Australia (1950-52).

MacDONALD, Sir John Alexander (1815-91) of Glasgow. First Prime Minister of Canada (1856). He was mainly instrumental in bringing about the confederation of Canada.

MacDONALD, Malcolm J., born 1901 in Lossiemouth. Son of Jas. Ramsay MacDonald. High Commissioner, Canada (1941-46); Governor-General, Malaya and Borneo (1946-48); Commissioner-General, S.E. Asia (1948-55); High Commissioner in India (1955-60) and Special Representative H.M. Govt. in Africa (1966-69). He was also Governor and C-in-C, Kenya (1963).

MacDONALD, S. Douglas, born 1899 in Glen Urquhart, Inverness-shire. Air Vice Marshal, Head of Air Training Advisory Group N.A.T.O. (1952-54).

MacDONALD, Thomas C., born 1909. Air Vice Marshal (1961) and Principal Medical Officer, Tech. Training Command R.A.F. (1961-66).

MacDONELL of Glengarry (Aeneas R. Donald). Air Commodore, Appointed Director of Management and Work Study, Ministry of Defence, Air Force Dept. in 1960.

MacDOUGALL, Alastair Ian, born 1888, son of late Col. Jas. Mac-Dougall of Edinburgh. Major-General (1940), (Ret. 1944). Commanded Royal Scots Grays (1928-32). General Staff, War Office (1936-39). Deputy Chief of General Staff (1940).

MacDOUGALL, Sir Donald, born 1912 in Glasgow. Head of Govt. Economic Service and Chief Economic Adviser to the Treasury 1969—.

McDOUGALL, John B., born 1890 in Greenock. Sometime Chief of Tuberculosis Section, World Health Organization, Geneva and Consultant in Tuberculosis to Egyptian Govt.

McEACHERN, Sir Malcolm Donald (1852-1910) of Islay. Shipowner. Mayor of the City of Melbourne (1899-1900).

McEWEN, Sir John B. (1868-1948) of Hawick. Composer and Principal of the Royal Coll. of Music, London (1924-36).

MacEWEN, Sir William (1848-1924) of Rothesay. A founder of Asceptic surgery and pioneer in surgery of the brain and lung, and in orthopaedic surgery.

McFADZEAN, Frank, born 1915 in Glasgow. Economist. Joined the Shell Oil Co. in 1952 and became Chairman in 1972.

McFADZEAN, William H., Baron (life peer), born 1903 in Stranraer. A Chairman of British Insulated Callender Cables Ltd. 1954—. Director (1959) and Deputy Chairman (1968) Midland Bank. etc.

MacFARLANE, George G., born 1916 in Airdrie. Appointed Controller (research) Ministry of Technology in 1967.

MacFARQUHAR, Sir Alexander, born 1903, educ. Aberdeen and Cambridge. Director of personnel United Nations (1962-67). U.N. Sec-General's special adviser for civil affairs in the Congo (1960).

MacFARQUHAR, Colin (1745-93) of Edinburgh. Printer and co-founder of the Encyolopaedia Britannica.

McGAW, William Rankin, born 1900, educ. Glasgow. Director of Aircraft Equipment Production (1941), of Aircraft Supplies (General) (1946-48) and of Production (1948-52). Director-General, Aircraft Production, Min. of Supply (1952-61).

McGILL, Donald Fraser (1875-1962). Originator of the popular, comic and somewhat naughty post-cards.

McGILL, James (1744-1813) of Glasgow. Fur-trader. Founded McGill College, Montreal, (which became McGill University in 1821).

McGILLIVRAY, Alexander (?-d. 1793). Scotsman who became a Red Indian Chief in 1777.

McGLASHAN, Sir Alexander D., born 1901, educ. Perth. Rear Admiral (1951), (retired).

McGONAGALL, William (1830-1902) of Dundee. Writer of doggerel verse.

MacGREGOR, Alasdair Alpin, born 1899. Author and traveller. Explored MacDonnell Ranges in Central Australia (1952-53). Prolific writer, usually illustrated with his own photographs.

MacGREGOR, Sir Alexander S.M., born 1881 in Arbroath. Physician. Medical Officer of Health, Glasgow (1925-46). President, Society of Medical Officers of Health (1941-42).

MacGREGOR, Andrew, born 1897 in Crieff. Air Vice Marshal. Senior Air Staff Officer H.Q. No. 4 Gp. (1940-42); Air Officer Admin., North Africa (1942-44); A.O.C. No. 28 Gp. (1945-46) and A.O.A., H.Q. Fighter Commd., (1946-49).

MacGREGOR, Sir Gregor (?-d. 1845). A remarkable character who became a General in the Venezuelan army under Simon Bolivar.

MacGREGOR, J. Geddes, born 1909, son of the late Thos. Geddes MacGregor of Dundee. Dean of the Graduate School of Religion and Professor of Philosophy of Religion, Univ. of Southern California 1960—.

MacGREGOR, Lewis R., born 1886 in Aberfeldy. Director-General Commonwealth of Australia War Supplies Procurement Mission, Washington and Ottawa (1941-45). H.M. Australian Minister to Brazil (1945-49).

MacGREGOR, Robert B., born 1896, educ. Dunbar and Edinburgh. Retired as Senior Medical Officer, Malacca Agricultural Medical Board in 1958. Director, Medical Services, Straits Settlements and Adviser, Medical Services, Malay States 1940—.

MacHABENS, Johannes (?-d. 1557). A reformer of the clan MacAlpine who, from 1542 was Professor of Theology at Copenhagen.

McHARDY, William D., born 1911 in Banffshire. Professor of Hebrew, Oxford Univ., 1960—. Examiner, Univs. of Aberdeen, Cambridge, Durham, Edinburgh, Leeds, London, Oxford and Gold Coast Univ. Coll.

MacILWRAITH, Sir Thomas, born 1835 in Ayr. Became Prime Minister of Australia in 1879.

MacINNES, Helen C., of Helensburgh? Author. Wrote many novels including 'Above Suspicion' (1941), 'The Unconquerable', 'Friends and Lovers' (1947), and 'North from Rome' (1958).

McINTOSH, Alastair, born 1913 in Dundee. Principal Adviser to the High Commissioner, Aden (1963-64).

MacINTOSH, Duncan W., born 1904 in Inverness. Commissioner of Police, Hong Kong (1946-54), (Retired). Police Adviser to the Govt. of Iraq (1954-58) and to Govt. of Jordan 1962—.

MacINTYRE, Sir Donald, born 1891 in Glasgow. Minister of Finance, Federation of Rhodesia and Nyasaland (1953-62). Made a Freeman of the city of Bulawayo in 1955.

MacIVER, Robert M., born 1882 in Isle of Lewis. Professor of Political Philosophy and Sociology, Columbia Univ. (1929-50) Director, New York City Juvenile Delinquency Evaluation Project (1956-61) and President of the New School of Social Research (1963-65).

MacKAIL, John William (1859-1945) of Bute. Professor of Poetry at Oxford (1906-11). President of the British Acadamy (1932-33).

MacKAY, Alexander Murdoch (1849-90) of Rhynie, Aberdeenshire. Pioneer missionary to Uganda (1878-87).

MacKAY, Charles (1814-89) of Perth. Songwriter, and editor of the Illustrated London News (1848-59). New York correspondent of 'The Times' during the Civil War (1862-65). Two of his songs 'There's a Good Time Coming' and 'Cheer Boys Cheer' were extremely popular.

MacKAY, Dave, born 1934. Footballer, Team trainer and Manager of outstanding ability. Known as the 'Iron Man' of football. Has 22 Scottish Caps. Certainly one of football's all-time greats.

MacKAY, Donald M., born 1922 in Caithness. Granada Research Professor of Communications, Keele Univ. 1960—.

MacKAY, Sir Gordon, born 1914 in Aberdeenshire. General Manager, East African Railways and Harbours (1961-64). With the World Bank 1965—.

MacKAY, Hugh (1640?-1692) of Scourie, Sutherland. Was promoted Major-General by William of Orange in 1689.

MacKAY, James, Botanist? Discovered sources of the Mississippi and Missouri rivers in 1784.

MacKAY, Sir John, born 1912 in Blantyre. Chief Inspector of Constabulary for England and Wales. Was Chief Constable, Manchester, (1959-66).

MacKAY, John A., born 1889 in Inverness. President of Princeton Theological Seminary (1936-59). Moderator, General Assembly of Presbyterian Church in the U.S.A. (1953).

MacKAY, John M. (1856-1931) of Lybster, Caithness. Was Professor of History at Liverpool Univ. for thirty years.

MacKAY, Mary (1855-1924) of Perth. Novelist, who wrote under the name 'Marie Corelli'. With 'The Sorrows of Satan' (1895) she became the most popular novelist of her time in Britain.

McKELLAR, Kenneth, born 1927 in Paisley. Singer and concert artist. Principal tenor Carl Rosa Opera Co. (1953-54). His TV and radio programme 'A Song for Everyone' was very well received. Has had several successful Commonwealth tours.

MacKENZIE, Alexander (1822-92) of Perthshire. Canadian statesman. Prime Minister of Canada (1873-78).

MacKENZIE, Sir Alexander (1755?-1820) of Stornoway. Explorer in

N.W. Canada. Crossed the Rockies to the Pacific (1792-93). The MacKenzie river bears his name.

MacKENZIE, Charles Frederick (1825-62) of Peeblesshire. First Anglican Bishop in Central Africa.

MacKENZIE, Colin, born 1872 in Gairloch. Rear Admiral (Retired 1926).

MacKENZIE, Sir George (1636-91), educ. St Andrews and Aberdeen. Eminent lawyer and writer. Held the post of Lord-Advocate under Charles II and James II.

MacKENZIE, Sir George S. (1780-1848). Minerologist. First to obtain proof of the identity of diamond with carbon.

MacKENZIE, Sir Hugh, born 1913 in Inverness. Vice Admiral, Flag Officer Submarines (1961-63). Director, Atlantic Salmon Research Trust 1959—.

MacKENZIE, Sir James (1853-1925). Physician. Invented the Polygraph to record graphically the heart's action. Elected F.R.S. in 1915.

MacKENZIE, Sir Morell (1837-92). Physician and throat specialist, co-founder of the Hospital for Diseases of the Throat, London.

MacKENZIE, Sir Robert, born 1811 in Ross-shire. Prime Minister of Australia 1869.

MacKENZIE, William J.M., born 1909 in Edinburgh. Professor of Government, Glasgow Univ. 1966—. (Manchester Univ. 1949-66).

MacKENZIE, William Lyon (1795-1861) of Dundee. First Mayor of Toronto (1830). Elected to Legislature of Canada (1851).

MacKENZIE, William W. (1860-1924) of Scone. Lawyer and Industrial Arbitrator. Chairman, Railway National Wages Bd. (1920-26), Royal Commission on Licensing (1929-31) and on Newfoundland (1933). Chairman Royal Society of Arts (1937-38).

MacKINNON, Donald M., born 1913 in Oban. Professor of Divinity, Cambridge Univ. 1960—. Lecturer on Philosophy and Religion.

MacKINNON, Quintin (? -d.1892) of Argyll. Surveyor and explorer. Discovered MacKinnon's Pass in New Zealand about 1888.

MacKINNON, Sir William (1823-93). Founder of the British E. Africa Co.

MacKINTOSH, Angus M., born 1915 in Inverness. British High Commissioner in Ceylon and Ambassador to the Republic of Maldives 1969—.

MacKINTOSH, Charles (1766-1843) of Glasgow. Manufacturing Chemist. In 1823 gave his name to Syme's method of water-proofing, and the 'Mackintosh' raincoat emerged.

MacKINTOSH, Charles Rennie (1868-1928) of Glasgow. Architect, who exercised considerable influence on European design.

MacKINTOSH, Elizabeth (? -d.1952) of Inverness. Novelist and playwright. Under her pen-name 'Gordon Daviot' she wrote her best known novel 'Kip' (1929).

MacKINTOSH, Sir James (1765-1832) of Aldourie, Loch Ness. Journalist, Historian, Philosopher and Statesman. Professor of Law at East India Coll. Haileybury (1818-24).

MacLAREN, Sir Hamish, born 1898 in Banffshire. Director of Electrical Engineering, Admiralty (1945-60).

McLAREN, Hugh C., born 1913 in Glasgow. Professor of Obstetrics and Gynaecology, Univ. of Birmingham 1951—.

McLAUGHLIN, John. A Scottish chemist in Toronto. Invented the popular soft drink 'Canada Dry' about 1890.

MacLAURIN, Colin (1690-1746) of Kilmodan, Argyll. Mathematician. His treatise on Fluxions (1752) was of great importance. Was also the Author of 'A Treatise on Algebra'. Elected F.R.S. in 1719.

MacLEAN, Alistair, born in Glasgow. Novelist and Playwright. His 'H.M.S. Ulysses', 'The Guns of Navarone', 'Where Eagles Dare' are only three of his many exciting books. One of the world's most successful adventure writers. Has had 16 of his novels made into films. Describes himself as a business man whose business is writing.

MacLEAN, Allan, born 1840. Statesman. Became Prime Minister of Victoria, Australia in 1899.

MacLEAN, Sir Charles H. Fitzroy, Baron (life peer). Chief Scout of the British Commonwealth and Empire (1959-71).

MacLEAN, Donald M., born 1899 in Isle of Lewis. Commodore Capt., Cunard Fleet and Commander R.M.S. Queen Elizabeth (1960-62).

MacLEAN, Sir Harry (Kaid) (c. 1848-1920) of Mull. Sometime Commander-in-Chief of the Sultan of Morocco's Army.

McLEAN, Sir Kenneth G., born 1896, educ. Edinburgh. Lieut-General, Deputy Adjutant-General G.H.Q. Far East (1945-46). Chief of Staff C.C.G. and Deputy Military Governor British Zone, Germany (1949), Chief Staff Officer Min. of Defence (1951-52).

McLEAVE, Hugh, born 1923 in Kilwinning, Ayrshire. Author, linguist and traveller. Invited in 1957 by Brit. Govt. to report on an H-bomb test over Christmas Island. His novel 'The Sword and the Scales' (1967) is popular.

MacLELLAN, George D., born 1922 in Glasgow. Professor and head of Engineering, Univ. of Leicester 1965—. Visiting Professor Michigan State Univ. (1955-58).

MacLENNAN, Sir Ian, born 1909 in Glasgow. Appointed British High Commissioner in New Zealand in 1964.

MacLEOD of Fuinary, Baron, born 1895. Lecturer on Evangelism. First holder of Fosdick Professorship (Rockefeller Foundation) Union Theological Seminary, New York (1954-55).

MacLEOD, Ian Norman (1913-1970). Politician and Cabinet Minister. Minister of Health (1952-55) of Labour and National Service (1955-59); Sec. of State, Colonies (1959-61); Chairman Conservative Party (1961-63); Editor of 'The Spectator' (1963-65) and Chancellor of the Exchequer when he died.

MacLEOD, John J.R. (1876-1935) of Cluny. Physiologist. Professor of Physiology at Cleveland (1903), Toronto (1918). Celebrated for his work on the isolation of insulin.

MacLEOD, Norman (1812-72) of Campbeltown. Divine and writer. Appointed Chaplain to Queen Victoria in 1857.

McLEOD, Walter, born 1887, educ. Edinburgh. Emeritus Professor, Univ. of Leeds 1952—. Produced several publications on Bacteriology.

MacLURE, William (1768-1840). Made a fortune as a merchant in London, and later settled in the U.S.A. Carried out a geographical survey of the U.S.A., crossing the Allegheny mountains 50 times. Published the results in 1817 in the 'Transactions of the American Philosophical Society!'

MacMILLAN of MacMILLAN, Sir Gordon H.A., born 1897. General,

G.S.O. 2 War Office and Eastern Command (1937-40); G.S.I. (1940-41); Brigade General Staff U.K. and N. Africa (1941-43); Commander, Infantry Bde., Sicily (1943), 15th Scottish and 51st Highland Divs. (1943-45); G.O.C. Palestine (1947-48); C-in-C, Scottish Command and Gov. of Edinburgh Castle (1949-52) and Governor and C-in-C Gibraltar (1952-55).

MacMILLAN, Harold, born 1894, of Scottish descent, (his paternal grandfather was a West Highland crofter). Prime Minister of Gt. Britain (1957-63). The standard of living rose at a greater rate during his administration than at any other time in British history. Known as 'Super Mac' he is also remembered for his 'Wind of Change' warning on Africa.

MacMILLAN, Kirkpatrick (1813-78) of Thornhill, Dumfriesshire. Invented the first cycle to be propelled by cranks and pedals (1838-39). A replica of the machine can be seen in the Science Museum, South Kensington. He was fined 5/- (the first recorded cycle fine) for knocking over a child.

MacMILLAN, Norman, born 1892 in Glasgow. Author. Was pilot of the first attempt to fly around the world (1922); First flight London to Sweden in one day; Chief Test Pilot, Fairy Aviation Co. (1929-30) and Armstrong Siddeley Development Co. (1931-33). Produced many publications on flying.

MacMILLAN, Roddie, of Anderston, Glasgow. Actor on Screen and TV. Popular as the detective in the TV series 'The View from Daniel Pyke'.

MacMURRAY, John, born 1891 in Maxwellton. Lecturer on Philosophy Univ. of Manchester (1919); Professor at University of Witwatersrand, Johannesburg, and Professor of the Philosophy of mind and logic at the Univ. of London (1928-44).

MacNAB of MacNAB, Archibald C., born 1886. Commissioner at Rawalpindi (1934); Administrator, Jahore (1937); Commissioner, Jullundur (1940) and Financial Commissioner Punjab (1945).

MacNAB, George H., born 1904 in Edinburgh. Surgeon. Sometime at Westminster Hospital and the Hosp. for Sick Children, Gt. Ormond Street.

McNAUGHT, John (1813-81) of Paisley. Inventor of the Compound Steam Engine.

MacNEIL of BARRA (Robert Lister) born 1884. Chairman of

Inventions Board, British Purchasing Commission, U.S.A. and founder of American Committee for Defence Of British Homes (1939-45). Boston Univ. Resident Architect (1949-51).

McNEILL, Alister A.C., born 1884, educ. Glasgow. Major-General (1941). Hon. Surgeon to the King (1935-43).

McNEILL, Florence M., of Orkney. Author, journalist, lecturer and broadcaster.

McNEILL, Sir James, Chief designer of R.M.Ss 'Queen Mary' and 'Queen Elizabeth' for John Brown of Clydebank.

McPETRIE, James Stewart, born 1902 in Aberdeenshire. Director-General of Electronics Research and Development at Min. of Aviation (1958-62). Director Racal Electronics (1965-69).

MacPHERSON, Sir David Lewis (1818-96) from near Inverness. Politician and Canadian Railway Builder.

MacPHERSON, Sir Hubert Taylor, (1827-86). Major-General at Tel-el-Kebir (1882).

MacPHERSON, James (1736-96) of Ruthven. Poet and translator. Appointed Surveyor-General of the Florides (1764), and in 1779 Agent to the Nabob of Arcot. Buried in Westminster Abbey.

MacPHERSON, Sir John (1745-1821) of Sleat, Isle of Skye. Appointed Governor-General of India in 1785.

McPHERSON, Sir John, born 1898 in Edinburgh. Colonial servant and businessman. Governor of Nigeria (1948-54) and Governor-General, Federation of Nigeria (1954-55). Permanent Under-Sec. of State for the Colonies (1956-59).

MacQUARIE, Lachlan (1761-1824) of Isle of Ulva. Major-General and Governor of New South Wales, Australia (1809-21). Sometime affectionately called the 'father of Australia'.

MacRAE, James (c.1677-1744) of Ayrshire. Governor of Madras 1725-30.

McROBERT, Sir George R., born 1895 in Aberdeen. Consulting Physician, Hosp. for Tropical Diseases, London Univ. Coll. Hospital.

MacTAGGART, Sir Andrew, born 1888 in Ayrshire. Civil Engineer. Was responsible for the construction of hydro-electric developments in Italy, India and East Africa, and the construction of large irrigation and railway works in Iraq.

McVEY, Sir Daniel, born 1892 in Falkirk. Sometime Chairman Dunlop Rubber Australia Ltd., and British Aircraft Corp. (Australia) Ltd. and several other Companies.

McVITTIE, George C., born 1904, educ. Edinburgh and Cambridge. Professor of Astronomy, Univ. of Illinois 1952–. Sec. American Astronomical Society 1961–. Published several books on Cosmology.

McWHIRTER, Robert, born 1904 in Glasgow? Professor of Medical Radiology. Lecturer, American Rontgen Ray Society (1963).

MAIR, William (1830-1920) of Aberdeenshire. Divine and writer. A pioneer in church reunion.

MAITLAND, Alastair G., born 1916. Director-General of Trade Development, British Consulate, New York 1968–.

MAITLAND, Donald J. Dundas, born 1922. Ambassador to Libya 1969–.

MALCOLM, Sir John (1769-1833) of Langholm. Soldier and Diplomat. Three times Ambassador to Persia, (1800, 1807 and 1810). Governor of Bombay (1826-30).

MANSON, George (1850-76) of Edinburgh. Painter and wood engraver.

MANSON, Sir Patrick (1844-1922) of Old Meldrum. The father of tropical medicine. The first, jointly with Sir Ronald Ross, to discover that parasites were transmitted by insects. He was sometimes known as 'Mosquito Manson'.

MARSHALL, William Calder (1813-94) of Edinburgh. Sculptor (R.A. 1852) of memorial statues and busts, including the group 'Agriculture' on the Albert Memorial.

MARTIN, Martin (?-d.1719) of Skye. Author and traveller. His book 'A Description of the Western Isles' aroused Dr Johnson's interest in the country.

MARTIN, Sir Theodore (1816-1909) of Edinburgh. Man of Letters. Became a Parliamentary solicitor in London. Was requisitioned by Queen Victoria to write the 'Life of Prince Consort' (5 vols. 1874-80).

MASSON, David (1822-1907) of Aberdeen. Scholar and literary critic. The biographer of Milton. His 'Life of John Milton' (6 vols. 1859-80) has been described as the most complete biography of any Englishman.

MATHIESON, William A.C., born 1916. Sometime Minister of Education, Labour and Lands, Kenya. Deputy Sec. Min. of Overseas Development 1968—.

MATTHEWS, James, born 1889 in Perthshire. Professor of Botany Univ. of Reading (1929-34), Univ. of Aberdeen and Keeper of Cruickshank Botanic Gardens (1934-59).

MAUCHLINE, Rev John, born 1902. Professor of Old Testament Language and Literature. Principal Pollock lecturer at Pine Hill Divinity Hall, Halifax, Nova Scotia 1949—.

MAXTON, James (1885-1946) of Glasgow. Chairman, Independant Labour Party (1926).

MAXWELL, Sir Aymer, born 1891 in Kirkcudbrightshire. Major-General (retired 1944). Chairman British Legion, Scotland (1954-58). Member of the Queen's Body Guard for Scotland, (The Royal Company of Archers).

MAXWELL OR CLERK-MAXWELL, James Clerk (1831-79) of Edinburgh. Physicist. First Professor of Experimental Physics at Cambridge (1871). He first forecast the possibility of radio transmission (1865). Invented Automatic control system (1868), and was creator of the electro-magnetic theory of light.

MAXWELL, Sir John, born in Ayrshire? 1882. Chief Constable of Manchester (1927-43).

MAXWELL, Sir Willwood G.C., born 1882, son of late Geo. Maxwell of New Galloway. Rear Admiral (1934), (retired). Recalled as Flag Officer, Tyne Area (1939-46).

MEIKE, David E.C., born 1902, educ. Edinburgh. Professor of Clinical Surgery and Surgery, Univ. of Malaya (1935-55). Surgeon, Singapore General Hosp. and Hon. Surgical Consultant, Far East Command.

MEIKLE, Andrew (1719-1811) from near Dunbar. A prolific inventor. Threshing machines (1784), Fantail gear (1750) and Governing sails (1772) for windmills were only three of his inventions.

MELVILLE, Andrew (1545-1622?) of Montrose. Presbyterian theologian. In 1568 became a professor at Genoa. Was repeatedly Moderator of the General Assembly.

MELVILLE, Archibald, born 1912 in Edinburgh. Appointed Director of Agriculture, Kenya in 1960.

MELVILLE, Sir Harry, born 1908, educ. Edinburgh and Cambridge. Appointed Sec. to the committee of the Privy Council for Scientific and Industrial Research in 1956. Member, Governing Bd. of National Institute for Research in Nuclear Science 1957—.

MELVILLE, Herman (1819-91), New York son of a Scottish merchant. Novelist and poet. Remembered for his famous 'Moby Dick' (1851) which came to be regarded as one of the greatest novels of American literature.

MELVILLE, Thomas (1726-53) of Glasgow. Scientist. Was the first (1752) to study the spectra of luminous gases.

MENZIES, Andrew, Invented horse and man-powered coal-cutting machines in 1863.

MENZIES, Sir Laurence J., born 1906, son of late Jas. Menzies, of Cupar-Angus. Appointed Adviser to the Governors of the Bank of England in 1957.

MENZIES, Sir Robert, born 1891 in Edinburgh. President Upper India Chamber of Commerce (1939-41 and 44-45); Chairman, Federation of Woollen Manufacturers in India (1941-47) and other Companies.

MENZIES, Sir Robert, born 1894 in Japarit, Australia, of Scottish descent. Prime Minister of Australia (1939-41 and 49-66).

MENZIES, Thomas, born 1893 son of late T. Menzies of Cults, Aberdeenshire. Professor of Tropical Medicine, Royal Army Medical Coll. (1940). Major-General (1949). Served R.A.M.C. in 1914-18 and 39-45 wars. Director of Medical Services, G.H.Q. M.E.L.F. (1948-50). Hon. Physician to the King (1949-52).

MERCER, Sir Walter, born 1890 in Midlothian. Emeritus Professor of Orthopaedic Surgery, Fellow, Royal Society of Medicine and Assoc. of Surgeons, Gt. Britain and Ireland.

MICHIE, Charles W., born 1907, educ. Aberdeen. Permanent Sec. to N. Region, Ministry of Agriculture in Nigeria (1957-60). Consul for Spanish Territories of Gulf of Guinea, and Labour Officer. Nigerian Dept., of Labour (1940-42).

MICKLE, William Julius (1735-88) of Langholm. Poet. Best remembered for 'There's nae luck aboot the hoose'.

MILL, James (1773-1836) from near Montrose. Philosopher, editor and writer. Wrote 'History of British India' (1817-18). Appointed Asst., Examiner with charge of the Revenue Dept. of the East India Co. (1819) and in 1832 head of the Examiners Office where he had control of all the departments of Indian Administration.

MILL IRVING, David J., born 1904 in Edinburgh. Ambassador to Costa Rica (1956-61). Special Ambassador for the inauguration of the President of Honduras (1957) and of Costa Rica (1958).

MILLAR, Betsy (1793-1864) of Saltcoats, Ayrshire. First woman ever to be registered at Lloyd's as a ship's Captain.

MILLAR, Hugh (1802-56) of Cromarty. Man of Letters, Geologist, writer and editor. 'Old Red Sandstone' (1841) is considered his best geological work.

MILLAR, Patrick (1731-1815) from near Dumfries. Inventor and projector of steam navigation.

MILLAR of ORTON, Robert Kirkpatrick, born 1901 in Morayshire. Major-General, Commanded Royal Engineers 15th (Scottish) Div. (1942-45) in France and Germany. Chief Engineer, London District (1949-51); Scottish Command (1951-53). Engineer-in-Chief, Pakistan Army (1953-57).

MILLAR, William (1838-1923) of Thurso. Missionary to India. Founder of Madras Christian College.

MILLER, Sir James, born 1905 in Edinburgh. Architect. Lord Provost of Edinburgh (1951-54) and Lord Mayor of London (1964-65).

MILLER, Maxwell of Glasgow. In 1850 invented an improved still for distilling and rectifying spirits.

MILLER, William (1810-72) of Glasgow. Poet. 'Wee Willie Winkie' is one of his best known poems about children and childhood.

MILN, James (1819-81). Antiquary. Made excavations at a Roman site at Carnac, Brittany (1872-80). 'Miln' Museum, Carnac contains the collection.

MILNE, Alasdair, born 1930 in Aberdeen. Controller B.B.C. Scotland (1968-72). Appointed Director of Programmes B.B.C. Television in

1973.

MILNE, Alexander, born 1891 in Skene, Aberdeenshire. Engineer, engaged from 1927 on opening up and development of Cochin harbour, S. India. Chief Engineer Cochin harbour (1941-48).

MILNE, Sir David (1763-1845) of Edinburgh. Admiràl known as 'The Hero of Algiers'. Was C-in-C Plymouth (1842-45).

MILNE, William (1785-1822) of Kinnethmont, Aberdeenshire. Missionary in China.

MILNE, William (1815-63) son of the above William. Was also a missionary in China.

MILNE, William P., born 1881 in Longside, Aberdeenshire. Professor of mathematics, Univ. of Leeds (1919-46).

MILNE HENDERSON, Capt. Thomas M.S., born 1888 in Edinburgh. Surveyor in charge of Marine Survey of India (1930-35). Appointed Capt. Supt., H.M. Indian Naval Dockyard Bombay and Chief of Staff R.I.N. in 1937.

MINTO, William (1845-93) of Alford, Aberdeenshire. Critic and Biographer. Went to London and became editor of 'The Examiner'. He also wrote for the 'Daily News' and 'Pall Mall Gazette'.

MITCHELL, Arthur J., born 1893, educ. Montrose. Civil Engineer, Director Colonial Development Corp. (1949-51). Regional Controller, C.D.C. for Central Africa and the High Commission Territories (1951-53).

MITCHELL, Sir Thomas Livingstone (1792-1855) of Craigend, Stirlingshire. Explorer and Surveyor. Governor-General of New South Wales 1823–. In four expeditions (1831, 1835 and 1845-47) he did much to explore Eastern and tropical Australia.

MITCHISON, Naomi M., of Edinburgh. Novelist. 'The Conquered' (1923); 'When the Bough Breaks' (1924) and 'Cloud Cuckoo Land' are three of her best works.

MOFFAT, James (1890-1944) of Glasgow. Theologian. Held Professorships at Mansfield Coll. Oxford (1911-14); the U.F. Church Coll., Glasgow (1914-27) and the Union Theological Seminary New York (1927-39).

MOFFAT, Robert (1795-1883) of Ormiston, E. Lothian. Missionary and explorer in Africa. He printed both New (1840) and Old (1857) Testaments in Sechwana language. David Livingstone married his daughter.

MOIR, John C., born 1900 in Montrose. Professor of Obstetrics and Gynaecology at the Univ. of Oxford 1937—. Visiting Professor, Queen's Univ. Ontario (1950).

MOIR, Percival J., born 1898, educ. Glasgow. Professor of Surgery and Dean of the Faculty of Medicine, Univ. of Leeds (1952-60), (retired).

MOLESWORTH, Mary (1839-1921), born in Rotterdam of Scottish descent, her maiden name being Stewart. Novelist and writer of Children's books. 'The Carved Lion' (1895) considered by many to have been her best. In all she wrote over a hundred books.

MOLLISON, James Allan (1905-59) of Glasgow. Airman. Won fame for his record flight, Australia to England in 1931. Made the first solo East-West crossing of the North Atlantic in 1932, and in 1933 the first England to South America flight.

MONBODDO, (James Burnett) Lord (1714-99) of Kincardineshire. Judge, philosopher and philologist. Wrote 'An Essay on the Origin and Progress of Language' (6 vols. 1773-92) and 'Ancient Metaphysics' (6 vols. 1779-99).

MONRO, Alexander (I), (1697-1767). Anatomist. One of the founders of the Edinburgh Infirmary.

MONRO, Alexander (2), (1733-1817) of Edinburgh, son of (I). Anatomist, succeeded his father. Wrote on the Nervous System (1783), the Physiology of fish (1785) and on the brain, eye, and ear (1797). Was the first (1767) to describe and use a stomach tube.

MONRO, Alexander (3), (1773-1859) son of (2). Anatomist, succeeded his father. Wrote on Hernia, the stomach and human anatomy. Elected F.R.S. of Edinburgh.

MONTGOMERY, James (1771-1854) of Irvine. Poet and journalist. Started and edited the 'Sheffield Iris' (1794-1825). He was also a hymn writer, the best being 'For Ever with the Lord'.

MONTROSE, (James A. Graham) 7th Duke of, born 1907. Minister of Agriculture, Lands and Natural Resources in Southern Rhodesia (1964) and Minister of External Affairs and Defence, S. Rhodesia (1966-68).

MONTROSE, (James Graham) 1st Marquis of (1612-50). Soldier and Statesman. Wrote a number of lyrics, the best known of which is 'My Dear and Only Love'.

MOODIE, Donald (? -d.1861) of Melsetter, Orkney. Naval Commander. Colonial Secretary at Natal (1845-51).

MOORE, Sir John (1761-1809) of Glasgow. General. Distinguished himself in the descent upon Corsica (1794). Served in the West Indies (1796); Ireland (1798); Holland (1799); Egypt (1801); Sicily and Sweden (1802) and Spain (1808-09).

MORAY, (James Stuart) Earl of (1531-70). Appointed Regent of Scotland (1567) and was one of the Commissioners sent to England to conduct negotiations against Mary Queen of Scots.

MORISON, Robert (1620-83) of Aberdeen. Botanist and Physician. Sometime in charge of the gardens of the Duke of Orleans. Charles II made him one of his physicians. Botanist Royal and Professor of Botany at Oxford.

MORRISON, Alexander, born 1917, educ. Edinburgh. Controller of Services, Greater London Council 1970—. Executive Director Highways and Transportation (1967-69) and other appointments in Stores Control and Supply.

MORRISON, Charles, of Greenock. Surgeon. Was in 1753 the first projector of the Electric Telegraph.

MORRISON, George (c. 1704-99). General, Military Engineer and Quartermaster-General.

MORRISON, John, born 1906 in Lanarkshire. Sometime Professor of Mechanical Engineering at Univ. of Bristol.

MORRISON, Robert (1782-1834) from near Jedburgh. Missionary. In 1818 established the Anglo-Chinese College at Malacca. Completed in 1823 his great Chinese Dictionary.

MORRISON, Stuart L., born 1922 in Glasgow. Professor of Social Medicine. Member of scientific staff, Medical Research Council, Social Research Unit (1956-62). Visiting Fellow, **Epidemiology** and Statistics, Univ. of N. Carolina (1961-62).

MORTON, Thomas (1781-1832). Shipbuilder and inventor (about 1822) of the patent slip which provided a cheap substitute for a dry-dock.

MOWAT, Sir Oliver (1820-1903) son of John Mowat a Freswick, Caithness soldier. A great advocate of the Union of Canada into a Dominion. Premier and Attorny-General of Ontario (1872-96) and Lieut-Governor 1897—.

MOWAT, Robert A. (1843-1925). Became a Judge of the Court of H.B. Majesty of Japan in 1891.

MUIR, Edwin (1887-1959) of Orkney. Poet and novelist. Published his first volume of verse in Prague (1925). Took over the British Institute in Rome (1948-50). Elected Professor of Poetry at Harvard (1955-56).

MUIR, Ernest, born 1880, educ. Edinburgh. Medical Missionary to U.F. Church in Kalna, Bengal (1905-20), Medical Supt. Leper Settlement, Chacachacare (1904-45).

MUIR, John (1838-1914) of Dunbar. Naturalist, explorer and conservationist. Known as the 'Father of United States Conservation'.

MUIR, John C., born 1902. Senior Agricultural Officer Zanzibar (1935), Director of Agriculture, Zanzibar (1941); Trinidad (1944) and Tanganyika (1948).

MUIRHEAD, David, born 1918 in Stirlingshire. Head of Personnel Dept., Foreign Office 1960—.

MUIRHEAD, John H. (1855-1940) of Glasgow. Philosopher. Editor of the 'Library of Philosophy' (1890) and Professor at Mersey Coll. Birmingham (1897-1921).

MUNRO, Ferguson R., Viscount Novar, born 1860. Governor-General of Australia (1914-20).

MUNRO, Sir Hector (1726-1805) of Novar. Soldier and General. Distinguished himself in India.

MUNRO, Hugh A.J. (1819-85) of Elgin. Classical scholar. Professor of Latin at Cambridge (1869-72).

MUNRO, Neil (1864-1930) of Inverary. Novelist and journalist. Remembered for his 'Para Handy' series, beginning with the 'Vital Spark' (1906).

MUNRO, Sir Thomas (1761-1827) of Glasgow. General. Served from 1780 as a soldier and administrator at Madras and was Governor from 1819 till his death.

MUNRO, William, born 1900 in Kilmarnock. Queen's Counsellor. Called to the Bar in the Straits Settlement (1927); Johore, Singapore and Malaya (1927-57).

MURCHISON, Sir Ronald Impey (1792-1871) of Terradale, Ross-shire. Geologist. His establishment of the Silurian system won him European fame. In 1844 he foreshadowed the discovery of gold in Australia. Was President of the British Assoc., in 1846 and for many years, of the Royal Geographical Society.

MURDOCH, Sir Walter, born 1874 in Aberdeenshire. Chancellor of the Univ. of Western Australia (1943-47); Lecturer, at the Univ. of Melbourne and leader writer in the 'Melbourne Argus'.

MURDOCK, William (1754-1839) of Old Cumnock, Ayrshire. A prolific inventor. In 1785 he invented a steam tricycle, Gas lighting from coal (1796-1803); a steam cannon (1803); Worm-driven cylinder-boring machine (1810) and a crown-saw boring machine. He also perfected underwater paint for ships.

MURRAY, Alexander (1775-1813) of Kirkcudbright. Philologist, he acquired a mastery of the classics. Became Minister of Urr in 1806 and Professor of Oriental languages, Edinburgh (1812).

MURRAY, Alexander S. (1841-1904). Sometime keeper of Greek and Roman Antiquities in the British Museum.

MURRAY, Charles (1864-1941) of Alford, Aberdeenshire. Civil Engineer. Was for some time, Chief Engineer and Secretary for Public Works in the Union of South Africa.

MURRAY, Colin R.B., born 1892 in Ross-shire. Deputy Director Intelligence, Govt. of India (1938) and Inspector-General of Police Orissa, India (1944-46).

MURRAY, Sir David (1849-1933) of Glasgow. Landscape painter (R.A. 1905).

MURRAY, Lord George (c.1700-60). Jacobite General. Joined the 'Young Pretender' in 1745.

MURRAY, Sir George (1772-1846) of Crieff. General, Statesman and writer. Sec. of State for the Colonies (1828-30). Was Major-General of the Ordnance till his death. Elected F.R.S. in 1824.

MURRAY, Sir Horatius, born 1903. General. Served with distinction in N. Africa, Sicily, Italy and France (1939-45). Commander, Commonwealth Div. in Korea (1953-54); G.O. C-in-C Scottish Commd.and Governor of Edinburgh Castle (1955-58). C-in-C Allied Forces, Northern Europe (1958-61), (retired).

MURRAY, James (c.1719-94) of Edinburgh. General. Became Governor of Quebec and of Minorca. Governor of Canada (1763-66).

MURRAY, or MURRAY PULTNEY, Sir James (c.1713-1811) of Fifeshire. (7th Baronet of Clermont). General and Statesman.

MURRAY, James, born 1919 in Isle of Arran? First Sec. (Information) British Embassy, Cairo (1949-54); Paris (1957-61). Ambassador to Rwanda and Burundi (1962-63). Consul-General, San Francisco 1970.

MURRAY, Sir James A.H. (1837-1915) of Denholm. Philosopher and Lexicographer. The editing of the Philological Society's 'New English Dictionary' (1879-1928) was the great work of his life.

MURRAY, James D., born 1911 in Edinburgh. Appointed British High Commissioner in Jamaica in 1965. Ambassador to Haiti 1966—.

MURRAY, John (1), (1745-93) of Edinburgh. Publisher in Fleet Street, London.

MURRAY, John (2), (1778-1843), son of (1). Carried on his father's business in London. He issued the travels of Mungo Park, Belzoni, Perry, Franklin etc.

MURRAY, John (3), (1808-92), son of (2). Issued the works of Livingstone, Darwin, Smiles, Smith's Dictionaries etc.

MURRAY, Sir John (c.1768-1827) 8th Baronet of Clermont. Soldier and General who distinguished himself in the Middle East.

MURRAY, Sir John (1841-1914), born in Canada of Scottish descent, and educated in Edinburgh. Marine Biologist and Oceanographer.

MURRAY or MORAY, Sir Robert (1600-73) of Perthshire. One of the founders of the Royal Society. Buried in Westminster Abbey.

MUTCH, James R., born 1905, educ. Aboyne. Air Commodore (1954) Engineer Specialist Officer, Director of Tech. Training, Air Ministry (1956-59)(retired). Was Senior Technical Staff Officer H.Q. Flying Training Command (1953-56).

MYLNE, Robert (1734-1811) of Edinburgh. Architect and Engineer. Designed Blackfriars bridge and planned the Gloucester and Berkeley ship canal. Elected F.R.S. in 1767. Was Surveyor of St. Paul's (1766-1811).

MYLNE, William Chadwell (1781-1863) son of Robert. Engineer Architect and Surveyor. Constructed many reservoirs and bridges.

N

NAIRN, Boyce J.M., born 1903. Consul-General, Tangier (1957-63).

NAIRN, Kenneth, born 1898 in Edinburgh. Air Vice Marshal. Chartered Accountant, served on Air Council as Air Member, Accounts and Finance (1939-44), then Special Adviser on Finance to Minister for Air.

NAIRNE, (Carolina Oliphant), Baroness (1766-1845) of Gask, Perthshire. Songwriter. Wrote 87 songs, at least four of which are immortal: 'Land O' the Leal', 'Caller Herrin', 'The Laird O' Cockpen' and 'The Auld Hoose'.

NAPIER, Sir Charles (1786-1860) from near Falkirk. Admiral of the Fleet of the Queen of Portugal, defeated the Mignelite fleet and placed Donna Maria on the throne. He also defeated Ibrahim Pasha in Lebanon, attacked Acre and blockaded Alexandria.

NAPIER, John (1550-1617) of Merchiston, Edinburgh. Mathematician. Invented Logarithms (1614) and civil engineering devices.

NAPIER, Sir Mellis, born 1882 in Dunbar. Chief Justice of Southern Australia (1942-67).

NAPIER, Robert (1791-1876) of Dumbarton. Shipbuilder and Engineer. Built the first four Cunard steamships and some of the earliest ironclad vessels.

NASMITH, David (1799-1839) of Glasgow. Philanthropist. Founded the City Missions in various cities in Europe and America.

NASMYTH, Alexander (1758-1840) of Edinburgh. Portrait painter of renown.

NASMYTH, James (1808-90) of Edinburgh. Engineer. Invented the steam hammer in 1839 and later a pile driver and a dentist's drill.

NASMYTH, Patrick (1787-1831) of Edinburgh. Son of Alexander. Landscape painter, sometimes called the 'English Hobbema'.

NEILL, Alexander S., born 1883 in Forfar. Author and child Psychologist. Produced many publications on child psychology.

NELSON, Sir Hugh, born 1835 in Kilmarnock. Elected Prime Minister of Australia in 1893.

NICHOLL, John, born 1894, educ. Stirling and Glasgow. Professor of English Language and Literature in the Univ. of Birmingham, and visiting Professor of English, Univ. of Pittsburg U.S.A. (1963-65 and 67-68).

NICHOLL, Sir William Robertson (1851-1923) of Lumsden. Man of Letters. Editor of 'The Expositor' the British Weekly (1886). Wrote books on Theory and Literature.

NICHOLSON, Peter, born 1765 in Preston Kirk. Became a distinguished mathematician and architect. Compiled an Architectural Dictionary.

NICOL, Cameron Macdonald, born 1891 in Aberdeen. Brigadier in Indian Medical Service. Director of Public Health, Punjab, (1936-41).

NICOL, William (c. 1768-1851), Inventor of the Nicol Prism which bears his name.

NIELSON, James Beaumont (1792-1865) of Shettleston. Invented the Hot Blast process in iron manufacture.

NINIAN, St. Lowland Scots Ringan (c. 360-432) from the shores of the Solway Firth. The first known Apostle of Scotland. Made a pilgrimage to Rome and was consecrated Bishop by the Pope.

NISBET, Stanley, born 1912 educ. Dunfermline and Edinburgh. Professor of Education, Univ. of Glasgow 1951–. Research Officer at the Air Ministry (1944-46). Lecturer on Education, Univ. of Manchester (1946) and Professor of Education, Queen's Univ. Belfast (1946-51).

NOBLE, Sir Peter, born 1899 in Aberdeen? Principal of King's Coll. Univ. London (1952-68). Sometime Governor of St Thomas's Hospital.

O

OGG, Sir William G., born 1891 in Cults. Director of Rothmanstead Experimental Station (1943-58). Sometime Foreign member of the All-union Academy of Agriculture Science in the U.S.S.R.

OGILBY, John (1600-76) of Edinburgh. Topographer, printer and Map-maker. Surveyor of the gutted sites after the Great Fire of London (1666). His more important maps and atlases included Africa (1670) and Asia (1673). His Road Atlas of Gt. Britain was unfinished (1675).

OGILVIE, Lady Mary, daughter of the late Prof. A. Macaulay of Glasgow. Principal of St Anne's Coll. Oxford 1953—.

OGILVY, Angus, born 1928. Company Director. Married H.R.H. Princess Alexandra of Kent. President, Scottish Wild Life Trust; Imperial Cancer Research Fund; British Rheumatism and Arthritis Assoc.; Chairman National Assoc. of Youth Clubs etc.

ORCHARDSON, Sir William Q. (1831-1910) of Edinburgh. Painter, of portraits and Industrial, and Social subjects. His 'Napoleon on board the Bellerophon' (1880) is in the Tate Gallery.

ORR, Robin, born 1909 in Brechin. Composer and Professor of Music, Cambridge Univ. and Fellow of St John's College 1965—.

OSWALD, Richard (1704-84) of Watten, Caithness. Appointed Plenipotentiary for Gt. Britain in 1782 and sent to Paris where he concluded a peace treaty with the U.S.A. which he signed with Benjamin Franklin.

OWEN, Robert Dale (1801-77) of Glasgow. Went to America in 1825 to help in the New Harmony colony. Edited the 'Free Inquirer' in New York, was a member of the Indiana Legislature and entered Congress in 1843. Was Minister at Naples (1853-58) and was an abolitionist and spiritualist.

P

PARK, Mungo (1771-1806) of Foulshiels, near Selkirk. Explorer in Africa and of the river Niger. Told his activities in 'Travels in the Interior of Africa' (1799).

PARKER, Agnes, born in Irvine. Artist and wood engraver. Walter Brewster prize winner at 1st International Exhibition of engravings and lithography, Chicago, (1929).

PATERSON, Arthur S., son of the late Prof. W. Paterson of Edinburgh. Physician in Charge, Dept. of Psychiatry, West London Hospital 1946—.

PATERSON, James R.K., born 1897. Professor of Radiotheraputics,

Univ. of Manchester 1960—. Director of Radiotherapy, Christie Hosp. and Holt Radium Inst. (1931-62).

PATERSON, Neil, born 1915, educ. Banff and Edinburgh. Author. Director, Grampion Television. Award winner, American Acadamy of Motion Picture Arts and Sciences (1960). His publications include; 'Behold Thy Daughter' (1950) and 'Man on the Tight Rope' (1953).

PATERSON, Robert (1715-1801) from near Hawick. The original 'Old Mortality', for over 40 years, devoted himself to repairing and erecting head-stones to Covenanting martyrs, neglecting his wife and five children.

PATERSON, William (1658-1719) of Dumfriesshire. Founder of the Bank of England and one of the first Directors in 1694.

PATERSON, William J.M., born 1911, educ. Glasgow. British Deputy High Commissioner, Madras 1961—. First Secretary, Beirut (1947-50). Damascus (1950), Santiago (1951-53), Foreign Office (1953-55), Counsellor, Baghdad and Oslo (1955-61).

PATON, George P., born 1882 in Angus. Commercial Consultant at Moscow (1930-37); Consul-General Istanbul (1937-42); Director, Intelligence Div., Far Eastern Bureau, British Min. of Information, New Delhi (1943-46).

PATON, Herbert J., born 1887 in Abernethy? Author and editor. Chairman, Board of the Faculty of Social Studies (1944-46), and of Bd. of Studies for Psychology (1950-52). Visiting Professor, Univ. of New York (1955).

PATON, John (?-d.1684) of Fenwick, Ayrshire. Covenanter who became a Captain in the army of Gustavus Adolphus.

PATON, John Gibson (1824-1907) of Dumfriesshire. Missionery to the New Hebrides in 1858.

PATON, Sir Joseph N. (1821-1901) of Dunfermline. Sculptor, painter and poet. R.S.A. and Queen's Limner for Scotland from 1865.

PATON, Robert, born 1894 in Perth. Consulting Surgeon (Retired). Medical Supt., St Mary's Hosp., Paddington (1924-27). Sometime Consulting Surgeon, Princess Louise Kensington Hosp. for Children.

PATON, William C., born 1886, educ. Glasgow and Edinburgh. Major-General (Ret.). Surgeon-General, Bengal (1941-45). Was Inspector-General of Civil Hospitals, N.W. Frontier Province (1939-41).

PATRICK, James M., born 1907, educ. Dundee and Glasgow. Painter and Etcher. Paintings purchased for National Galleries, Millbank, South Africa, Capetown and Southern Australia.

PAUL, John, (known as John Paul Jones) (1747-92) of Abigland near Kirkburn. Founder of the American Navy. He also served in the French Navy.

PENNEY, Jose' Campbell, born 1893, educ. Edinburgh. Was Political Adviser to British Admin. in ex-Italian colonies in Africa (1946-50); U.K. Representative on U.N. Consul for Libya (1950-51).

PENTLAND, (Henry John Sinclair) 2nd Baron, born 1909 in Lyth, Caithness. Sometime Director and Vice-President of the American British Elect., Corp. (New York) and of Hunting Surveys Inc. (New York).

PEPLOE, Samuel John (1871-1935) of Edinburgh. Artist whose still-life paintings brought him fame as a colourist.

PERTH, (John D. Drummond) 17th Earl, born 1907. Minister of State for Colonial Affairs (1957-62).

PETTIE, John (1839-93) of Edinburgh. Painter (R.A. 1873). His works, apart from portraits were mainly historical and literary subjects, and had considerable popularity.

PHILLIP, John (1817-67) of Aberdeen. Painter (R.A. 1859). Went to London in 1836.

PICKEN, Andrew (1788-1833) of Paisley. Author. Published a series of novels including 'The Sectarian' (1829); 'The Dominies Legacy' (1830) and 'Waltham' (1833).

PICKEN, Ebenezar (1769-1816) of Paisley. Poet. Published several volumes of Scots poems and a 'Pocket Dictionary of Scottish Dialect' (1818).

PIRIE, Norman W., born 1907 in Stirlingshire. Demonstrator in the Biochemical Laboratory, Cambridge (1932-40). Head of the Biochemistry Dept., Rothamstead Experimental Station, Harpenden 1947—.

PITCAIRN, Robert (1747-70). Scottish midshipman. Pitcairn Island is named after him because he was the first to have sighted it.

PITCAIRN, Robert (1793-1855) of Edinburgh. Antiquary.

PLAYFAIR, John (1748-1819) from near Dundee. Mathematician, Physicist and Geologist.

PLENDERLEITH, Harold J., born 1898, educ. Dundee. Director, International Centre for the study of the Preservation of Cultural Property (created by UNESCO) 1959—.

POLSON, William, of Paisley. About 1840 with John Brown produced a cornflour powder when they were trying to make starch for cloth from maize. Now Brown and Polson is part of a world-wide concern, marketing a large range of other food products.

PONT, Timothy (c. 1560-1630), educ. St Andrews. Geographer, Mathematician, Cartographer and Minister of Dunnet, Caithness (1601). Produced the first Scottish Atlas.

PORTEOUS, Alexander, born 1896 in Haddington. Professor of Education, Univ. of Liverpool (1954-63). Prof. of Philosophy at South Coll. Northampton, Mass. U.S.A. (1926-30) and at McGill Univ. Montreal (1930-32).

PORTEOUS, Rev. Norman, born 1898 in Haddington. Professor of Hebrew and Semitic Languages, Univ. of Edinburgh 1937—. Principal of New Coll. and Dean of the Faculty of Divinity, Edinburgh 1964—.

PRINGLE, Sir John, born 1707 in Stichill. Sometime Physician Extraordinary to the King.

PRINGLE, Thomas (1789-1834) of Blaiklaw. Writer. Was for three years, Govt. Librarian at Capetown. On his return to London he became Sec. to the Anti-slavery Society.

R

RAE, John (1813-93) from near Stromness, Orkney. Explorer and Arctic traveller. In 1848 he accompanied Richardson on a Franklin search voyage. Commanded an expedition (1853-54) to King William's Land, and in 1860 surveyed a telegraph line to America via Faroes and Iceland. In 1864 he made a telegraph survey from Winnipeg over the Rocky Mountains.

RAE, Sir Robert, born 1894. Director of the National Agricultural Advisory Service (1948-59). Agricultural Attaché, British Embassy, Washington (1944-45).

RAEBURN, Sir Henry (1756-1823) of Edinburgh. Famous Artist and portrait painter. Elected R.A. in 1815.

RAEBURN, John (1833-1909) of Fife. Violin maker, painter, astronomer and poet.

RAMSAY, Allan (1685-1758) of Leadhills. Pastoral Poet. Wrote 'The Gentle Shepherd', a pastoral comedy, (1725) and 'Thirty Fables' (1730) his most popular.

RAMSAY, Allan (1713-84), son of Allan of Leadhills. Portrait painter of distinction.

RAMSAY, Sir Andrew Crombie (1814-91) of Glasgow. Geologist. Appointed Director-General of the Geological Survey in 1871.

RAMSAY, Sir William (1852-1916) of Glasgow. Professor of Chemistry at Bristol (1880-87) and Univ. Coll., London (1887-1912). In conjunction with Lord Rayleigh he discovered Argon in 1894. Later he discovered Helium, Neon, Krypton and Xenon, and won a Nobel Prize in 1904.

RAMSAY, Sir William M. (1851-1939) of Glasgow. Archaeologist. An authority on Asia Minor, wrote 'A Historical Geography of Asia Minor' (1890).

RANDOLPH, Sir Thomas (? -d.1332). Soldier and Statesman and comrade of Bruce who created him Earl of Moray. He commanded a Division at Bannockburn; took Berwick (1318); won the victory of Mitton (1319); re-invaded England (1320 and 1327), and was Regent from Bruce's death (1329) until his own.

RANKIN, Henry C.D., born 1888 in Ayrshire. Major-General. Served with distinction in 1914-18 war. Surgeon to C-in-C, India (1923-25 and 27-31), Surgeon to the Governor, Bombay (1936-37). Deputy Director Medical Services in Indian Army Commands (1941-46).

RANKIN, Robert, born 1915, educ. Fettes and Cambridge. Professor of Mathematics, Glasgow Univ. 1954—. Prof. of Pure Mathematics at Birmingham Univ. (1951-54). Visiting Professor, Indiana Univ. (1963-64).

RANKINE, William J.M. (1820-72) of Edinburgh. Engineer and Scientist. His work on the steam engine, machinery, ship-building, applied mechanics, metal fatigue etc., became standard text-books. He it was who evolved the scientific term 'Energy'. Elected F.R.S. in 1853.

REDPATH, Anne, of Galashiels. Painter. One of the most important modern Scottish artists. Elected R.S.A. in 1952.

REID, Sir Alexander, born 1889, educ. Glasgow and Australia. Member of the Commonwealth Grants Commission 1954—. Under-Treasurer, Govt. of West Australia (1938-54).

REID, Archibald C., born 1915, educ. Edinburgh and Cambridge. Secretary for Fijian Affairs 1959—. Was British Agent and Consul in Tonga (1957).

REID, Sir Francis, born 1900 in Bearsden. Brigadier (1950) Commander, Ceylon Garrison and U.K. Troops in Ceylon (1949-50); Cyprus District (1950-51); Cyrenaica District (1951-52) and Ceylon Army (1952-55).

REID, Sir George (1841-1913) of Aberdeen. Painter of portraits and landscapes. R.S.A. (1877).

REID, James Scott Cunningham, Baron (life peer) of Drem, born, 1890 in E. Lothian. Lord of Appeal in Ordinary 1948—. Solicitor-General for Scotland (1936-41); Lord Advocate (41-45); Dean of the Faculty of Advocates (1945-48). Chairman, Malaya Constitutional Commission (1956-57).

REID, John, born 1906 in Callander. Chief Veterinary Officer, Ministry of Agriculture, Fisheries and Food 1965.

REID or ROBERTSON,John (1721-1807) of Perthshire. Soldier and musician. Entered the army in 1745 and rose to the rank of General.

REID, Louis A., born 1895 in Ellon. Professor of Philosophy of Education, Institute of Education, London Univ. (1947-62).

REID, Thomas (1710-96) of Strachan Manse. Eminent Philosopher. Wrote several books on metaphysical subjects including 'Essays on the Intellectual Powers' (1785).

REID, Sir William (1791-1858) of Kingussie. Meteorologist, soldier and administrator. Served with distinction in the Peninsular war, and was Governor of Bermuda, Windward Islands and Malta.

REITH, John Charles W., 1st Baron of Stonehaven (1889-1971). Known as the 'Father of the B.B.C.' (1927-38); Minister of Information (1940); Min. of Transport (1940); Min. of Works and Buildings (1940-42). First Chairman of B.O.A.C. (1939-40).

RENNIE, George (1791-1866) of Phantassie farm, East Linton. Engineer son of John (1761-1821). With his brother John carried on an immense business of shipbuilding, railways, bridges, harbours, docks, machinery and marine engines. Sometime Supt. of the machinery of the Royal Mint.

RENNIE, Sir Gilbert, born 1895, educ. Stirling and Glasgow. Governor and C-in-C, Northern Rhodesia (1948-54). High Commissioner in U.K. for Federation of Rhodesia and Nyasaland (1954-61).

RENNIE, John (1761-1821) of Phantassie farm, East Linton. Civil Engineer. Builder of bridges, canals and docks. Built some 60 bridges including Waterloo and Southwark. He built the London and East and West India Docks, and docks at Leith, Plymouth, Liverpool, Dublin, Hull, Chatham and Portsmouth. The Kennet and Avon Canal was also his work.

RENNIE, Sir John (1794-1874) son of John and brother of George. Was knighted on his completion of the construction of London Bridge in 1831.

RENWICK, William L., born 1889 in Glasgow. Professor of Rhetoric and English Literature, Univ. of Edinburgh (1945-49). Prof. of English Language and Literature, King's Coll. Newcastle-upon-Tyne in the Univ. of Durham (1921-45). Visiting Prof. China (1943-44).

RICHARDSON, Frank M., born 1904, educ. Glenalmond and Edinburgh. Major-General (1957). Director of Medical Services, B.A.O.R. (1956-61).

RICHARDSON, Sir John (1787-1865) of Dumfries. Naturalist, Physician and Arctic explorer. Commanded the expedition in search of Franklin (1848-49).

RIDDOCH, John, born in Edinburgh. Surgeon, Solihull Hosp., Warwickshire 1949—. Surgeon, Midland Hosp., Birmingham (1926-49) and Corbett Hosp. Stourbridge (1939-58).

RIDDOCH, John H., born 1909 in Gourock. Under-Sec. Ministry of Aviation 1962—.

RILEY, James, of Glasgow. Discovered Nickel-steel in 1889.

RITCHIE, Anthony E., born 1915, educ. Edinburgh and Aberdeen. Professor of Physiology, United Coll. of Univ. of St Andrews 1948—. Scientific Adviser, Civil Defence 1961—.

RITCHIE, Sir Douglas, born 1885 in Aberdeenshire. Chief Executive of London Port Emergency Committee (1939-46).

RITCHIE, Sir John, born 1904, educ. Turiff and Edinburgh. Principal and Dean of the Royal Veterinary Coll. Univ. of London 1965—.

RITCHIE, John K., 3rd Baron Ritchie of Dundee, born 1902. Chairman of the Stock Exchange (1959-65).

RITCHIE, Kenneth Gordon, born 1921 in Arbroath. Appointed High Commissioner in Guyana in 1967.

RITCHIE, Walter H.D., born 1901 in Perth? Major-General (1953) Director of Quartering, and of Supplies and Transport, War Office (1953-57).

RITCHIE, William (1781-1831) of Fifeshire. Solicitor and writer. One of the founders of the 'Scotsman' (1816-17).

RITCHIE-CALDER, Peter R., Baron (life peer), born 1906 in Forfar. Author, Scientific Social and Political journalist and Broadcaster. Director of Plans of Political Warfare in the Foreign Office (1941-45). Chairman, Metrication Bd. 1969—. Fellow of the World Acadamy of Arts and Science. Has written over 30 books which have been translated into more than 40 languages.

ROBB, Andrew M., born 1887, educ. Glasgow. Professor of Naval Architecture in Univ. of Glasgow (1944-57). Practiced as a consulting Naval architect (1925-44).

ROBB, James C., born 1924 in Inverurie. Professor of Physical Chemistry, Univ. of Birmingham 1957—.

ROBERTON, Sir Hugh (1874-1952) of Glasgow. Conductor of the Glasgow Orpheus Choir, which achieved international renown.

ROBERTSON, Archibald, born 1853 in Edinburgh. Divine. Bishop of Exeter (1903-16). Appointed Principal of King's College in 1897.

ROBERTSON, George C. (1842-92) of Aberdeen. Philosopher, became Professor of Mental Philosophy and Logic at Univ. Coll. London.

ROBERTSON, James (c. 1720-88) of Fifeshire. Soldier. Governor of New York (1779). Commander-in-Chief, Virginia (1780).

ROBERTSON, Sir James, born 1899 in Broughty Ferry. Governor-

General and C-in-C of the Federation of Nigeria (1955-60). Director of Uganda Co. 1961—, and other high offices in East Africa.

ROBERTSON, James, of Paisley. A grocer who founded what is now one of the largest preserve manufacturers in the world.

ROBERTSON, James C. (1813-82) of Aberdeen. Divine and Author of the 'History of the Christian Church'. Was appointed Canon of Canterbury in 1859.

ROBERTSON, John M., born 1900 in Auchterarder. Professor of Chemistry, Univ. of Glasgow 1942—. Director of Laboratories 1955—. Visiting Professor, Univ. of California, Berkeley, U.S.A. (1958). President, Chemical Soc. (1962-64).

ROBERTSON, John Mackinnon (1856-1933) of Arran. Politician, critic and editor of the National Observer in London (1891-93). Was Liberal M.P. for Tyneside and rose to be Secretary to the Board of Trade and a Privy Councellor.

ROBERTSON, Joseph (1810-66) of Aberdeen. Antiquary. Contributed much to Chamber's Encyclopaedia.

ROBERTSON, Dame Nancy. Commandant and Director of the Women's Royal Naval Service (1954-58).

ROBERTSON, William (1721-93) of Borthwick. Historian. His 'History of Scotland 1542-1603', (1759) was a great success, and was followed by the 'History of Charles V' (1769), his most valuable work for which he received £4,500 and high praise from Voltaire and Gibbon.

ROBERTSON, Sir William (1860-1933). Believed to be the only British soldier to rise from private to Field Marshal, (C.I.G.S. 1915-18).

RODGER, Thomas R., born 1878 educ. Lanark, Glasgow and Edinburgh. Aural Surgeon. Senior Surgeon, Ear Nose and Throat Dept., Hull Royal Infirmary (1919-38). Group Officer, Min. of Health (1939-46).

ROPER, Andrew, of Hawick. A farmer who in 1737 invented the winnowing machine.

ROSS, Alexander, born 1880 in Forres. Brigadier-General and Barrister. Judge of District Court of Yorkton, Saskatchewan (1921-55).

ROSS, Alexander D., born 1883 in Glasgow. Executive Officer, Pan Indian Ocean Science Assoc. Consultant, East-West Centre, Univ. of Hawaii, Honolulu (1961-64).

ROSS, Sir David, born 1877 in Thurso, Caithness. Chairman Civil Service Tribunal (1942-52) & Royal Commission on the Press (1947-49). Hon. Fellow of Merton, Balliol and Oriel Coll., and of Trinity Coll. Dublin.

ROSS, Sir David P. (1842-1904). Surgeon-General of British Guiana 1894—.

ROSS, Frank M., born 1891 in Glasgow. Chairman, Canadian Executive Committee and Joint Chief Executive, Lafarge Canada Co. Ltd. Sometime Director-General of Production of Naval Armaments and Equipment, Dept. of Munitions and Supply, Canada.

ROSS, Sir Hew D. (1779-1868) of Galloway. Field Marshal. Served with distinction under Wellington.

ROSS, James (1848-1913) of Cromarty. Civil Engineer. Constructed Railways in the U.S. and Canada. Built the mountain sections of the Canadian Pacific Rly. (1883-85). Financed and built, with others, Tramway systems in Montreal, Toronto, England, West Indies and Mexico.

ROSS, Sir James Clark (1800-62) born in London of Wigtownshire forebears. Discovered the Ross Sea which bears his name. He was also responsible for the establishment of the true position of the magnetic pole.

ROSS, James S., born 1892 in Brechin. Principal, Westminster Training College (1940-53). Lecturer on Education.

ROSS, Sir John (1777-1856) of Wigtownshire. Admiral and Explorer in Baffin Bay. Discovered the North West Passage to the pole. Was Consul at Stockholm (1839-46).

ROSS, Sir John Lockhart (1721-90) of Lanarkshire. Vice-Admiral, with distinguished service in the Channel and North Sea.

ROSS, Sir Ronald (1857-1932) born in India of Scots descent. Discovered that malaria parasites were carried by mosquitoes and transmitted to their victims while sucking blood.

ROSS, Sir William Charles (1794-1860). Painter. Painted many portraits of the Royal Family. Appointed miniature painter to the Queen in

1837.

RUDDIMAN, Thomas (1674-1757) of Banffshire. Grammarian and Philologist. Editor of Latin works.

RUSSEL, Alexander (1814-76) of Edinburgh. Journalist and editor of the 'Scotsman' from 1848. An antagonist of the Corn Laws.

RUSSEL, John Scott (1808-82) from near Glasgow. Engineer. Invented the 'Wave system' of Shipbuilding.

RUSSEL, Leonard J., born 1884. Professor of Philosophy, Univ. of Birmingham 1951—. Univ. of Bristol (1923-25).

RUTHERFORD, Charles (1858-1922) of Edinburgh. Principal Veterinary Officer, India (1908-13).

RUTHERFORD, Daniel (1749-1819) of Edinburgh. Physician and Botanist. In 1772 published his discovery of the distinction   between 'Noxious air' (nitrogen) and Carbon Dioxide.

RUTHERFORD, Ernest (1871-1937), New Zealand born of Scots descent. Physicist. Pioneer in Atomic research.

RUTHERFORD, John G. (1857-1923) of Peeblesshire. Sometime Commissioner, Board of Raily Comm. for Canada. Veterinary Director-General (1902-12) and Live Stock Commissioner (1906-12) for Canada.

RUTHERFORD, Samuel (1600-61) of Nisbet, near Jedburgh. Theologian and preacher. Professor of Divinity at St Andrews (1639). His chief fame rested upon his devotional works, such as 'Christ Dying and drawing sinners to Himself' (1649).

RUTHERFORD, Thomas W., (1832-1918) of Roxburghshire. Major-General in the Indian Army.

S

SCOTT, David (1806-49) of Edinburgh. Historical painter. His 'Vintager' is in the National Gallery. R.S.A. (1829).

SCOTT, Sir Ian D., born 1909 in Inverness. First Sec. Foreign Office (1950-51); British Embassy, Beirut (1954-59); Ambassador to Congo (1960-61), Sudan (61-62) and Norway (65-68).

SCOTT, John (1783-1821) educ. Aberdeen. Journalist. Became first editor of the 'London Magazine' in 1820.

SCOTT, John W., born 1878 in Lesmahagow. Professor of Logic and Philosophy, Univ. Coll. Cardiff (1920-44). Professor Emeritus since 1944.

SCOTT, Michael (c.1175-1230) of Balwearie. Scholar and Astrologer. Known as the 'Wondrous Wizard', became tutor and Astrologer at Palermo to Frederick II. He was one of the greatest scholars of his time, and his fame spread over Europe.

SCOTT, Michael (1789-1835) of Glasgow. Author. Spent some time in the West Indies. His 'Tom Cringle's Log' (1829-33) and 'The Cruise of the Midge' (1834-35) considered among his best works.

SCOTT, Paul H., born 1920 in Edinburgh. Consul-General, Vienna 1968—.

SCOTT, Sir Robert, born 1905 in Peterhead. Minister, British Embassy, Washington (1953-55). Commissioner-General for U.K. in S.E. Asia (1955-59). Permanent Sec. Min. of Defence (1961-63) retired.

SCOTT, Thomas, born 1897 in Montrose. Major-General. Chief of Staff to C-in-C Ceylon (1944); Director of Manpower Planning G.H.Q., India (1944-46); Deputy Chief of General Staff (B) G.H.Q., India (1946-47).

SCOTT, Sir Walter (1771-1832) of Edinburgh. Novelist, Poet, Historian, Antiquarian and Sheriff.

SCOTT ELLIOT, James, born 1902 in Dumfriesshire? Major-General (1954). G.O.C. 51st (Highland) Division (1952-56) retired.

SELKIRK, Alexander (1676-1721) of Largo, Fife. Sailor, whose story of his time on Juan Fernandez island is supposed to have suggested the 'Robinson Crusoe' of Defoe.

SELKIRK, Thomas Douglas, 5th Earl of (1771-1820). Explorer and colonizer. Settled emigrants from the Scottish Highlands in Prince Edward Island (1803) and Red River valley, Manitoba. Known as 'Selkirk of Red River'.

SEMPILL, Robert (c.1530-95). Author of witty and rather coarse ballads such as 'The Legend of a Lymaris Life' and 'Seige of the Castle of Edinburgh'.

SEMPILL, William F. Forbes-Sempill, 19th Baron., born 1893. A

Representative Peer for Scotland (1935-63). Royal Aeronautical Society Chairman (1926-27) and President (1927-30). Competed in the King's Cup Air Race 1924, 25, 26, 27, 28, 29 and 30.

SHARP, William (1855-1905) of Paisley. Novelist. Settled in London in 1879 and wrote on contemporary English, French and German poets, under the pseudonym 'Fiona Macleod'. He wrote some fine romances including 'The Mountain Lovers' and 'The Sin Eater' (1895), and 'The Immortal Hour'.

SHAW, Sir James (1764-1843) of Riccarton, Ayrshire. Was Lord Mayor of London in 1805.

SHEARER, Sir James G., born 1893 in Dundee. President of the Supreme Court, Asmara, Eritrea, (1953-62).

SHEARER, Moira, of Dunfermline. Actress and ballet dancer. Best remembered for her part as ballerina in the film 'The Red Shoes', (1948).

SHEPHERD, Rev. Robert H.W., born 1888 educ. St Andrews and Edinburgh. Missionary of U.F. Church of Scotland to S. Africa (1918), Cape Province (1920-26), Lovedale Missionary Institution (1927-58). President of the Christian Council of South Africa (1956-60).

SIBBALD, Sir Robert (1641-1722) of Edinburgh. Naturalist and Physician. Spent much time on Botany and Zoology. Was virtual founder of the Royal Coll. of Physicians, Edinburgh and became Scottish Geographer Royal.

SIM, Alastair, born 1900 in Edinburgh. Actor and Producer. Played leading roles in many popular films and on TV.

SIMMONDS, Kenneth W., born 1912 in Lanarkshire. Financial Sec. Nyasaland (1951-57) and Chief Secretary Aden (1957-63).

SIMPSON, Alfred H. (Mr Justice Simpson), born 1914 in Dundee. Puisne Judge, High Court of Kenya 1967—.

SIMPSON, Bill, born 1931 in Ayr. Actor. Became popular as Dr Finlay in the B.B.C. TV and Radio Series 'Dr Finlay's Casebook'.

SIMPSON, Sir George (1792-1860) actual place of birth in Scotland not certain. Canadian explorer and administrator (1821-56) of Hudson Bay Co. and its territory. Made an overland journey around the world in 1828. Simpson's Falls and Cape George Simpson are named after him.

SIMPSON, Sir James (1792-1868) of Roxburghshire. Soldier and General who served with distinction under Wellington.

SIMPSON, Sir James F., born 1874, educ. Falkirk and Glasgow. Chairman, Chamber of Commerce, Madras (1920-22). Sometime Governor of the Imperial Bank of India, and Consul for Norway at Madras.

SIMPSON, Sir James Young (1811-70) of Bathgate. Obstetrician and Professor of Midwifery. Discovered Chloroform in 1847, having experimented on himself. Surgeon to the Queen in Scotland (1847).

SIMPSON, William Douglas, born 1896 in Aberdeen. Librarian and Archaeologist. Directed excavations at many old Castles between 1919 and 1935 including Kildrummy, Kindrochit, Esslemont and Finavon.

SIMSON, Robert (1681-1768) of Glasgow. Mathematician. His great work was his restoration of Euclid's lost treatise on Porisms (1776).

SINCLAIR, Allan F.W., born 1900 in Edinburgh. Journalist and publicist. Editor of the 'Sunday Graphic' (1931-36) and 'Daily Sketch' (1936-39). Sometime Director British Information Services, Middle East. Specialist Radio Photographic Adviser India and Ceylon (1945). Joined the 'Daily Herald' in 1946 and later the 'Sun'.

SINCLAIR, Sir Archibald H.M., 1st Viscount Thurso of Ulbster, born 1892. Leader of the Liberal Party (1935-45); Sec. of State for Air in the Churchill Administration (1940-45).

SINCLAIR, Hugh M., born 1910 in Edinburgh. Fellow and Lecturer in Physiology and Biochemistry, Magdalen Coll. Oxford 1937–. Produced many publications on nutrition and metabolism.

SINCLAIR, James, 14th Earl of Caithness (1824-81). Patented many ingenius inventions, including a Loom, Steam Carriage, and Gravitating Compass.

SINCLAIR, John, (Lord Pentland) 1st Baron (1866-1925) from Edinburgh. Governor of Madras (1912-19). Secretary for Scotland (1905-12).

SINCLAIR, Sir John of Ulbster (1754-1835) from Thurso. Politician and Agriculturist. Founded the Board of Agriculture in 1793. Compiled the 'First Statistical Account of Scotland' (1791-99). Was undoubtedly one of the most energetic and enterprising Scotsmen who has ever lived.

SINCLAIR, Robert J., 1st Baron of Cleeve, born 1893, educ. Glasgow and Oxford. President, Imperial Tobacco Co. Ltd. 1959–. (Chairman 1947-59). Director-General of Army Requirements, War Office (1939-42).

SKENE, William Forbes (1809-92) of Inverie, Knoydart. Historian and close friend of Scott. Became Scottish Historiographer in 1881.

SKINNER, James Scott (1843-1927). Violinist, known as 'The Strathspey King'.

SKINNER, John (1721-1807) of Birse, Aberdeenshire. Historian and song-writer. Wrote the 'Ecclesiastical History of Scotland' (1788) and several songs of which 'The Ewie wi' the crookit horn' and 'Tullochgorum' were the best known.

SLESSOR, Mary (1848-1915) of Dundee. Missionary in Calabar, Africa for many years.

SLOAN, Sir Tennant, born 1884 of Glasgow. Joint Sec. Home Dept. Govt. of India (1932-36). Adviser to the Governor, United Provinces (1939-45).

SMEATON, John (1724-92) born near Leeds. A descendant of an old Perthshire family named Smeton. Civil Engineer. Builder of Bridges, Canals and Lighthouses. The Eddystone light revolutionised lighthouse design.

SMILES, Samuel (1812-1904) of Haddington. Author, Social reformer and physician. Became a surgeon in Leeds and editor of the 'Leeds Times', and in 1854, Secretary of the S.E. Railway.

SMITH, Adam (1723-90) of Kirkcaldy. Political economist and philosopher. Wrote 'The Wealth of Nations' in 1776. Regarded as the 'father' of the science of Political Economy.

SMITH, Alexander (1829-67) of Kilmarnock. Poet and novelist. His first publication 'A Life Drama' (1853) was very popular.

SMITH, James (1789-1850) of Deanston, Perthshire. Agricultural Engineer and Philanthropist. The inventor of 'Through Drainage' by means of a subsoil plough.

SMITH, James D.M., born 1895, educ. Aberdeen. Financial Sec.

Singapore (1947-51); U.N. Technical Assistance Administrator, Nicaragua (1953-55); Brazil (1957-58) and Venezuela (1959-61).

SMITH, Norman Kemp (1872-1958) of Dundee. Philosopher and Professor of Psychology (1906) and of Philosophy (1914) at Princeton U.S.A.

SMITH, Robert A., born 1909 in Kelso. Professor of Physics, Sheffield Univ. (1961-62). First Director, Centre of Materials Science and Engineering, Mass. Inst. of Technology (1962-68).

SMITH, Walter Chalmers (1824-1908) of Aberdeen. Poet who attained a considerable reputation. He was also a minister of the Free Church of Scotland. His works included 'The Bishop's Walk' (1861) and 'A Heretic' (1890).

SMITH, Sir William Alexander (1854-1914) of Pennyland, Thurso. Founder in 1883 of the Boy's Brigade.

SMITH, William Robertson (1846-94) of Keig, Aberdeenshire. Theologian and Orientalist. In 1883 he became Professor of Arabic at Cambridge. University Librarian and Adams Prof. of Arabic (1889). Chief editor of the Encyclopaedia Britannica 1887—.

SMOLLET, Tobias George (1721-71) of Dumbartonshire. Novelist. Sailed as a surgeon's mate on the expedition to Carthagena (1741). Practised in London as a surgeon. His literary work had mixed reception, and he was nicknamed 'Smelfungus' by Sterne.

SNELL, John (1629-79) of Ayrshire. Philanthropist. Founder of the Snell exhibition at Balliol Coll. Oxford.

SOMERVILLE, née Fairfax, Mary (1780-1872) of Jedburgh. Mathematician and scientific writer. Wrote 'Celestial Mechanism' in 1830. Somerville College Oxford is named after her.

SOUTER, William (1898-1943) of Perth. Poet. His best works included 'In the time of Tyrants' and 'The Expectant Silence'. His collection 'Seeds in the Wind' (1933) and 'Poems in Scots' (1935) gave him a place in Scottish literature.

SPENCE, Sir Basil U., born 1907 in India, of Scottish descent. Professor of Architecture, Royal Acadamy. Designed the new Coventry Cathedral (1951) and many other outstanding architectural masterpieces.

SPENCE, Lewis T. Chalmers (1874-1955) of Broughty-Ferry. Anthropologist, Author, Poet and Editor. His 'The Gods of Mexico' (1923) is a standard work.

SPOTTISWOOD, John (1565-1639) of Midcalder. Prelate and historian. Sometime Archbishop of Glasgow and St Andrews, and in 1635 Lord Chancellor of Scotland.

SPOTTISWOODE, Alicia Ann (Lady John Scott), (1810-1900) of Lauder. Poetess, Composer and Author. Her best remembered song is 'Annie Laurie'.

STAIR, John Dalrymple (1673-1747) **2nd Earl of,** born in Edinburgh. Soldier. Was Aide-de-Camp to Marlborough in 1703. Distinguished himself at Onderarde (1708) and Malplaquet. Promoted Field Marshal in 1742 and became Governor of Minorca.

STEIN, Jock, of Lanarkshire. Manager of Celtic, one of Britain's most successful football teams.

St. CLAIR, A. (c. 1734-1818) of Thurso. Soldier. A Lieutenant under General Wolfe, carried the colours on the Plains of Abraham. Sometime adviser to General Washington. Was elected President of Congress and Government of North West Territories.

STEELE, Sir John (1804-91) of Aberdeen. Sculptor. His best work, the equestrian statue of the Duke of Wellington (1832) and that of Prince Albert (1876) in Edinburgh.

STEPHEN, Robert A., born 1907, educ. Aberdeen. Major-General (1961), Director of Army Surgery and Consulting Surgeon to the Army, R.A.M.C. College (1959-67).

STEVENSON, Dorothy E. of Edinburgh, Cousin of R.L. Stevenson. Author of novels and children's verse. Her best known novels include 'Mrs Tim of the Regiment' (1932) and several other 'Mrs Tim' books.

STEVENSON, Robert (1772-1850) of Glasgow. Builder of Lighthouses (Including Bellrock). Invented the Flashing system. Was also a consulting engineer for roads, bridges, harbours, canals and railways.

STEVENSON, Robert Louis Balfour (1850-94) of Edinburgh. Novelist and Poet. His romantic thriller 'Treasure Island' (1883) was his most famous. 'Kidnapped' (1886); 'The Master of Ballantrae' (1889); 'Catrina' (1893) and many others were and still are very popular.

STEVENSON, Robert S., born 1889 in Edinburgh. Consultant Ear Nose and Throat Surgeon, Colonial Hosp. Gibraltar 1954—. Lecturer in

Chicago (1948); Toronto (1952); Bristol (1955); London (1956); Philadelphia (1957) and Yale Univ. (1958).

STEWART, Alexander B., born 1908, educ. Broughty-Ferry. Medical Adviser to the Greater London Council 1965—.

STEWART, Alexander Boyd., born 1904 in Tarland. Director of Macaulay Institute for Soil Research, Aberdeen 1958—.

STEWART, Alexander D., born 1883 in Blairgowrie. Sometime Director of All India Institute of Hygiene, Calcutta.

STEWART, Alexander T. (1803-76). American born Scot who became a millionaire and philanthropist.

STEWART, Alfred (1880-1947) of Glasgow. Scientist and writer of detective stories. Sometime Professor of Chemistry at Queen's Coll. Belfast. His stories include 'Murder in the Maze', 'The Case with Nine Solutions' and 'The Boat House Riddle'.

STEWART, Andy, of Arbroath. Singer, Composer, Comedian and broadcaster. Well known as host on TV's popular show 'The White Heather Club'. His recording of 'A Scottish Soldier' sold over a quarter of a million copies.

STEWART, Charles Edward Louis Philip Casimir (1720-88). The 'Young Pretender'. In the 1745 rising took Carlisle and advanced as far as Derby, but was crushingly defeated at Culloden Moor in 1746.

STEWART, Dugald (1753-1828) of Edinburgh. Professor of Moral Philosophy. His works include 'Philosophy of the Human Mind' and 'View of the Active and Moral Powers of Man' (1828).

STEWART, Francis Teresa, Duchess of Richmond and Lennox (1647-1702), daughter of Lord Blantyre. Described by Pepys as the greatest beauty he ever saw in his life. She posed for the effigy of Britannia on the coinage.

STEWART, George G., born 1919, educ. Glasgow. Commissioner for Forest and Estate Management, Forestry Commission 1969—.

STEWART, Sir Houston (1791-1895) of Ardgowan. Appointed Admiral of the Fleet in 1872.

STEWART, Sir Iain, born 1916, educ. Glasgow. Director, Beaverbrook Newspapers Ltd., B.E.A.; Eagle Star Ins. Co. Ltd.; Royal Bank of Scotland Ltd.; Lyle Shipping Co. Ltd. and other Companies.

STEWART, John I.M., born 1906 near Edinburgh. Scholar and detective story writer. Appointed in 1935 to the Chair of English at Adelaide University. His detective stories were written under the name 'Michael Innes' and the most successful included; 'Seven Suspects' (1936) and 'Lament for a Maker' (1939).

STEWART, John (Jackie) Young, born 1939 at Milton, Dumbarton-shire. Grand Prix Motor racing driver. World Champion 1969, 71 & 73. Runner up 1972. Retired from motor racing 1973.

STEWART, Sir William (1774-1827) of Galloway. Soldier, became Lieut-General and served with distinction under Wellington.

STEWART, William A.C., born 1915 in Glasgow. Professor of Education, Univ. of Keele 1950—. Visiting Professor McGill Univ., and Univs. of California and Manchester.

STEWART, William Ross, born 1889 in Edinburgh. Major-General. Surgeon to the Viceroy of India (1933-36). Deputy Director Medical Services, Ceylon Commd. H.Q. (1942-44) and to North Command, India (1945-46).

STIRLING, James H. (1820-1909) of Glasgow. Idealist, Philosopher and Lecturer. His 'Secret of Hepel' (1865) introduced that Philosopher's system into Britain and was a masterly exposition.

STIRLING, Rev Robert (1790-1878) of Perthshire. Invented a type of gas-sealed internal combustion engine in 1817. Taken up in 1972 by the Ford Motor Co. in connection with the development of a low pollution engine.

STIRLING, William (1851-1932) of Grangemouth. Professor of Physiology and History, Victoria Univ. Manchester. Sometime Professor of Physiology, Royal Institute of London.

STIRLING-ANSELAN, John B. (1875-1936) of Stirlingshire. Admiral. Served in China during the Boxer Rising (1900). Admiral Supt. Chatham Dockyard (1927-31).

STIRLING-MAXWELL, Sir William (1818-78) of Keir? Historical writer, Art critic and Virtuoso.

STRACHAN, John (1778-1867) of Aberdeen. Minister, became the first Bishop of Toronto in 1839.

STRANG, William (1859-1921) of Dumbarton. Painter and Illustrator. Was an Etcher of World class.

STRANGE or Strang, Sir Robert (1721-92) of Kirkwall. Line engraver with a European reputation. He was made a member of the Acadamies of Rome, Paris, Florence, Bologna and Palma (1760-65).

STRATH, Sir William, born 1909, educ. Glasgow. Sometime Chairman British Aluminium Co. Ltd., and several other Companies. Served in the Ministry of Aircraft Production, Min. of Supply, and the Treasury (1940-55). Member of Atomic Energy Auth., (1955-59) and Permanent Sec. Min. of Aviation (1959-60).

STRATHALMOND, (William Fraser) 1st Baron of Pumpherston, born 1888. Chairman of British Petroleum Co. Ltd. (1941-56). Director, Burma Oil Co. Ltd., and National Provincial Bank Ltd., etc.

STRATHCLYDE, (Thomas D. Galbraith) 1st Baron of Barskimming, born 1891. Under Sec. of State for Scotland (1945 and 51-55) Chairman North of Scotland Hydro-Elect. Bd. 1959—.

STRATHCONA, (Donald A. Smith) 1st Baron (1820-1914) from Forres. Canadian Statesman. Chief promoter of the Canadian Pacific Rly. (1885). High Commissioner for Canada in London (1896).

STRATHNAIRN, (Hugh Rose) 1st Baron (1801-85) born in Berlin, soldier son of Scottish Diplomat, Sir George Rose. He virtually re-conquered central India, and succeeded Lord Clyde as Commander-in-Chief, India (1860-65). He held the same post in Ireland (1865-70).

STUART, Sir Alexander (1825-86) of Edinburgh. Prime Minister of New South Wales, Australia, (1883-85).

STUART, John, 3rd Earl of Bute (1713-92) First Scottish Prime Minister of Great Britain (1762-63).

STUART, John McDougall (1815-66) of Dysart. Engineer, Surveyor and Explorer in Central Australia. Mount Stuart is named after him.

SUTHERLAND, Alexander (1852-1902) of Glasgow. Australian journalist. Mathematical Master in the Scotch College Melbourne (1875-77) and Principal of Carlton Coll. Melbourne (1877-92).

SUTHERLAND, Donald (1835-1919) of Wick, Caithness. Known as 'The Hermit of Milford Sound' in New Zealand. Discovered Sutherland Falls (one of the world's highest) which bears his name at Milford Sound. Sometime served in Italy with the forces of Garibaldi.

SUTHERLAND, George A., born 1891 in New Deer, Aberdeenshire.

Principal of Dalton Hall Univ. of Manchester (1924-58). Lecturer on Physics in London and South Africa.

SUTHERLAND, Sir Gordon, born 1907, in Watten, Caithness. Professor of Physics at Univ. Coll. Michigan (1949-55). Master of Emmanual College Cambridge 1964—.

SUTHERLAND, James (1849-1905) born in Canada, son of Alexr. Sutherland of Caithness. Became Minister of Public Works in Canada.

SUTHERLAND, James R., born 1900 in Aberdeen. Professor of Modern English Literature, Univ. Coll. London (1951-67).

SUTHERLAND, John (1808-91) of Edinburgh. Promoter of sanitary science. Was sent to Crimea (1855) to inquire into the sanitary conditions of British soldiers.

SUTHERLAND, Sir Thomas (1834-1922) of Aberdeen. Retired in 1914 as Chairman P & O Steam Navigation Co. and of the London Board of Suez Canal Co. Sometime Director of the London City and Midland Bank and Chairman, Marine and General Assurance Society.

SWAN, Annie Shepherd (1860-1943) from near Gorebridge. Novelist. Wrote 'Aldersyde' (1883) and a great number of popular novels.

SWINBURNE, Sir James (1858-1958) of Inverness. Electrical engineer. Took out over 100 patents during his lifetime. Was an accomplished musician and set two of Tennyson's poems to music. Elected Fellow of the Royal Society.

SYME, David (1827-1908) of North Berwick. Australian newspaper proprietor and economist.

SYME, James (1799-1870) of Edinburgh. Famous surgeon in his day. Professor of Clinical Surgery, wrote on Pathology, Stricture, Fistula, incised wounds etc.

SYMINGTON, William (1763-1831) Millwright and inventor. Built one of the first steamboats in 1788. It had two paddle-wheels in the middle of the deck. Inventor of a horizontal direct-acting engine which he fitted in the steam tug "Charlotte Dundas" in 1801. He died in poverty in London.

T

TAIT, Archibald Campbell (1811-82) of Edinburgh. Became Archbishop of Canterbury in 1869. He did much to extend and improve the organization of the church in the Colonies.

TAIT, Sir James S., born 1912, educ. Glasgow. Principal, Northampton Coll. of Advanced Technology, London (1957-66).

TAIT, Peter Guthrie (1831-1901) of Dalkeith. Mathematician, Philosopher and Physicist. Professor of Mathematics at Belfast (1854). Produced the first working Thermo-electric diagram. Published many papers on scientific subjects.

TAIT, William (1792-1864). Publisher and founder Tait's Edinburgh Magazine (1832-64).

TANNAHILL, Robert (1774-1810) of Paisley. Poet. Best remembered for his 'Bonnie Woods O' Craigie Lea' and 'Jessie the Flower O' Dumblane'.

TASSIE, James (1735-99) of Pollokshaws. Famed for his paste and imitation Gems. Was commissioned by Catherine the Great of Russia to supply her with some 15,000 items of imitation gems and cameos. The collection was put on exhibition to the general public before being sent to the Empress.

TAYLOR, Sir George, born 1904, educ. Edinburgh. Director of the Royal Botanic Gardens, Kew (1956-71). Joint leader of the British Museum Expedition to Ruwenzori and mountains of East Africa (1934-35) and to S.E. Tibet and Bhutan (1938).

TAYLOR, William, born 1892 in Banffshire. Under-Sec. Min. of Labour and National Service (1946-52). U.K. Delegate, International Labour Conference, Geneva (1949).

TELFORD, Sir Thomas (1757-1834) of Langholm. Civil Engineer. Builder of bridges, aquaducts, canals and docks. The Menai Suspension Bridge was perhaps his greatest work (1825). Buried in Westminster Abbey.

TEMPLETON, John (1802-86) of Riccarton near Kilmarnock. Tenor and operatic singer of renown. Was popular in London and New York.

TENNANT, Charles (1768-1838) of Ochiltree, Ayrshire. Pioneer chemical industrialist. Developed and manufactured a bleaching powder.

THOM, Alexander, born 1894, educ. Glasgow. Professor of Engineering Science at Oxford University (1945-61).

THOM, Herbert J., born 1895, educ. Edinburgh. Chairman, Traffic Commissioners Licensing Auth. for Goods Vehicles, South East Traffic Area. Regional Traffic Commissioner, (1953-65).

THOM, James, born 1910, educ. Edinburgh. Director of Forestry for England (1963-65), Director of Research (1965-68).

THOMAS the RHYMER, or Thomas Rymour of Erceldoune (c. 1220-97) of Berwickshire. Seer and poet. Said to have predicted the death of Alexander III and the battle of Bannockburn. His prophecies were collected and published in 1603.

THOMPSON, Sir D'Arcy W. (1860-1948) of Edinburgh. Marine Biologist and Zoologist. His 'Study on Growth and Form' (1917) had considerable merit.   Other works include papers on fishing and oceanography. Leader of the 'Challenger' expedition.

THOMPSON, John M., born 1887 in Rothesay. Professor of Botany at the Univ. of Liverpool (1921-52).

THOMSON, Adam, of Glasgow. Chairman of British Caledonian Airways 1972—, Britain's largest private airline.

THOMSON, Sir Charles W. (1830-82) of Linlithgow. Zoologist. Held Professorships in Natural History at Cork, Belfast and Edinburgh. Famous for his deep-sea researches, described in 'The Depths of the Oceans' (1872). Elected F.R.S. in 1869.

THOMSON, Daniel, born 1912 educ. St Andrews and Edinburgh. Civil Service Medical Adviser 1968—. Treasury Medical Adviser (1965-68).

THOMSON, David, born 1912 in Edinburgh. Professor in Public Law and Government, Columbia Univ. New York (1950-53) and member of the Institute for Advanced Study, Princeton (1950). Master of Sidney Sussex Coll. Cambridge 1957—.

THOMSON, George, born 1921 in Monifeith. Minister of State, Foreign Office (1964-66); Sec. of State for Commonwealth Affairs (1967-68); Shadow Defence Minister (1970). Appointed joint Commissioner to European Community (1972).

THOMSON, James (1700-48) of Roxburghshire. Poet whose best known work is 'Rule Britannia' (1740). Was Surveyor-General of the Leeward Islands (1739).

THOMSON, James (1768-1855) of Crieff. Sometime editor of the 'Encyclopaedia Britannica'.

THOMSON, James (1834-82) of Port Glasgow. Poet of very considerable merit. 'City of Dreadful Night' was his greatest work.

THOMSON, James N., born 1888, educ. Edinburgh. Major-General (1942). Asst. Master-General of the Ordnance in India (1934-37); Deputy Master-General of Ordnance, G.H.Q. India (1943). A.D.C. to the King in 1939.

THOMSON, Rev James S., born 1892, educ. Glasgow. Moderator, United Church of Canada (1956-58). Lecturer in Philosophy of Education, McGill Univ. 1959—.

THOMSON, John (1778-1840) of Ayrshire. Painter, who was one of the first landscape painters in Scotland. Was greatly admired by Sir Walter Scott who described him as one of the warmest-hearted men living.

THOMSON, Sir John A. (1861-1933) of Pilmuir, East Lothian. Scientist. Published many popular works, some of the best known being, 'The Wonder of Life'; 'Outline of Science' and 'Scientific Riddles'.

THOMSON, Joseph (1858-95) of Dumfriesshire. Geologist and Explorer in Tanganyika (1878-79) and Masai country (1883-84). Explored Southern Morocco for the Geographical Society in 1888.

THOMSON, Sir Landsborough, born 1890 in Edinburgh, Chairman, Public Health Laboratory Service Board (1950-61), of Home Office Advisory Committee on the Protection of Birds 1954—. President British Ornothologists Union (1948-55) etc.

THOMSON, Robert William (1822-73) of Stonehaven. Civil Engineer and expert on blasting. He was also an inventor. Designed improved machinery for making sugar in Java, invented a mobile steam crane and in 1845 the first rubber tyre, but it was considered a curiosity and not developed. India rubber was very expensive at that time as well.

THOMSON, Ronald B., born 1912 in Aberdeen. Air Vice-Marshal, Air Officer Admin., Flying Training Commd., 1963—. A.O.C.-R.A.F. Gibraltar (1958-60), Scotland and Northern Ireland (1960-63). Member of the Queen's Body Guard for Scotland (The Royal Company of Archers).

THOMSON, Roy H. 1st Baron of Fleet, born 1894 in Toronto, son of a Scottish barber. Newspaper and Television magnate. In 1959 became one of Britain's leading newspaper proprietors with the acquisition of the Kemsley Newspapers.

THOMSON, Thomas (1773-1852) of Crieff. Chemist. When making investigations in brewing and distillation, he invented the instrument known as Allan's Saccharometer.

THOMSON, Thomas (1817-78) of Glasgow. Surgeon and Naturalist. Discovered Pectic acid in carrots.

THOMSON, Thomas D., born 1911 in Edinburgh. Retired as Commissioner for Social Development, Nyasaland in 1963. Carried out a Survey of Adult Education in Nyasaland (1956-57), and organized Nyasaland Council of Social Service (1959).

THOMSON, William (1819-90) of Whitehaven, of Scottish parents. Became Archbishop of York.

THORBURN, Archibald (1860-1935) of Edinburgh? Artist who specialized in wild-life paintings. Exhibited at the Royal Academy (1880-1900).

TODD, Sir Alexander R., born 1907 in Glasgow. Chemist. Professor at Manchester (1938) and Cambridge (1944). Nobel Prize winner (1957) for his researches on vitamins B and E. Elected F.R.S.

TROTTER, Alexander C., born 1902 in Edinburgh. Editor of the 'Scottish Daily Express' (1934-59), and Chairman, Beaverbrook Newspapers (1959-70).

TROUP, Sir James A.G., born 1883 in Broughty-Ferry. Vice-Admiral (1939). Rear Admiral, Director of Naval Intelligence (1935-39).

TULLOCH, John (1823-86) of Bridge of Earn. Theologian. Prof. of Divinity at St Andrews (1854). Founded the Scottish Liberal Church Party in 1878.

TURNBULL, Sir Hugh S., born 1882, educ. Edinburgh. Commissioner of Police for the City of London (1925-50).

TURNER, Sir William, born 1907 in Kelso. Lieut-General (1956). O.C. 5th and later 1st K.O.S.B. (1942-46). G.S.O. 1, Middle East and Gt. Britain (1947-50). G.O.C.-in-C, Scottish Commd. and Governor of Edinburgh Castle (1961-64). Member of the Queen's Body Guard for Scotland (The Royal Company of Archers).

TWEED, John (1869-1933) of Glasgow. Sculptor. His principal works; the Cecil Rhodes memorial at Bulawayo, the completion of Steven's

Duke of Wellington at St Paul's and 'Clive' in Whitehall.

TWEEDSMUIR, John N.S. Buchan, 2nd Baron of Elsfield, born 1911. Served with distinction in the Canadian army (1939-45). President, Commonwealth and British Empire Chamber of Commerce (1955-57). President, Institute of Export 1963–.

TWEEDSMUIR, Priscilla J.F. Buchan, Baroness (life peeress) of Belhelvie. From Potterton, Aberdeen. Member of State at the Foreign Office. Leader of Delegation to Iceland on fishing limits dispute 1972–. Was U.K. Delegate to U.N. General Assembly (1960-61).

TYLER, William (1711-92) of Edinburgh. Historian, Lawyer and Writer. 'An Inquiry into the Evidence against Mary Queen of Scots' (1759) was his work.

U

URE, Andrew (1778-1857) of Glasgow. Chemist. Sometime Prof. of Chemistry and Natural Philosophy at Anderson's College and Analytical Chemist to the Board of Customs, India (1834). Produced a 'Dictionary of Chemistry' (1821) and was elected F.R.S. in 1822. Was the inventor of the Alkalimeter (1816) and a Bi-metal Thermostat in 1830.

URE, David (?-d.1798) of Glasgow. Geologist. Was employed by Sir John Sinclair in his preparation of the Statistical Account of Scotland.

URE, Mary, of Glasgow. Actress. Played leading parts in many films and on Television. Her films include; 'Look Back in Anger', 'Sons and Lovers', 'Where Eagles Dare', and 'The Mindbenders'. TV appearances include 'Honour thy Father and thy Mother'.

URQUHART, Sir Andrew, born 1918, educ. Greenock and Glasgow. Deputy Governor, Eastern Region, Nigeria, (1958-63). General Manager, The Housing Corp. (1964-70).

URQUHART, David (1805-77) of Cromarty. Diplomatist, writer and politician. Founded the 'Free Press' afterwards called the 'Diplomatic Review'. Wrote 'The Pillars of Hercules' (1850) in which he suggested the introduction of Turkish Baths into Britain.

URQUHART, Sir Robert W. born 1896, educ. Aberdeen. Appointed Inspector-General of H.M. Consular Establishments in 1945; Minister at Washington (1947); at Shanghai (1948-50) and Brit. Ambassador to Venezuela (1951-55).

URQUHART, Sir Thomas (1611-60) of Cromarty. Author and devoted warrior for Charles I and II. Known for his brilliant translation 'Rabelais'. Said to have died from a fit of laughter on hearing of the restoration of Charles II.

V

VEDDER, David (1790-1854) of Deerness, Orkney. Poet, who was also a sailor and Customs Officer.

VEITCH, John (1829-94) of Peebles. Author. Professor of Logic and Rhetoric at St Andrews (1860). His works include 'Lives of Dugald Stewart' (1857); 'Sir W. Hamilton' (1869) and 'Tweed and other Poems' (1848).

VEITCH, William (1794-1885) from near Jedburgh. Classical scholar. His chief work was the invaluable 'Greek Verbs Irregular and Defective' (1848).

VEITCH, William, born 1885, in Edinburgh. Director of Kemsley Newspapers (1937-57).

VEITCH, William L.D., born 1901, educ. Edinburgh. Major-General. Commanded the Bengal Sappers and Miners (1943-46). Engineer-in-Chief, Pakistan Army (1950-53), retired.

W

WADDELL, Sir Alexander, born 1913 in Angus. Colonial Sec. Gambia (1952-56); Sierra Leone (1956-58). Governor and C-in-C, Sarawak (1960-63).

WALKER, Sir James (1863-1935) of Dundee. Chemist. Known for his work on hydrolysis, ionization and amphoteric electrolytes. Elected F.R.S. in 1900.

WALKER, James, born 1916, educ. Falkirk. Professor of Obstetrics and Gynaecology. Visiting Prof. Univ. of New York State (1957); Florida (1965) and McGill Univ. (1967).

WALKER, Sir William, born 1905 in Fifeshire. Chairman, Jute Industries Ltd. Dundee (1968-70). Many Directorships in Industry, Shipping and Banking.

WALLACE, Alfred Russel (1822-1913) of Usk. Scientist who independently formulated Darwin's theory of natural selection.

WALLACE, Sir Donald M. (1841-1919) of Dumbartonshire. Journalist, traveller and foreign correspondent of 'The Times'. Edited 10th edition of Encyclopaedia Britannica.

WALLACE, Ian B., born in London of Scottish parents. Singer, Actor and Broadcaster. Panellist on radio quiz game 'My Music'. Theatrical career includes a Royal Command Performance in the Palladium (1952) and 'Toad' in 'Toad of Toad Hall' (1964).

WALLACE, John B., born 1907 in Cambusland. Air Vice-Marshal. Deputy Director-General of Medical Services, R.A.F. (1961-66).

WALLACE, Robert (1773-1855) of Ayrshire. Parliamentarian, Postal and Law reformer. It was mainly through him that Rowland Hill's penny postage was introduced.

WALLACE, Sir William (1274-1305) from near Paisley. Scottish patriot and hero. Chief champion of Scotland's independence.

WALLACE, William (1844-97) of Cupar. Became Professor of Moral Philosophy at Oxford.

WALLACE, William (1860-1940) of Greenock. Composer. Wrote a Symphony, Symphonic poems, songs and works on music.

WALLS, Eldred W., born 1912 in Glasgow. Professor of Anatomy in Univ. of London at Middlesex Hosp. Medical School 1949–, (Dean, 1967–.)

WALLS, Henry, born 1907, educ. Edinburgh. Director, Metropolitan Police Laboratory, New Scotland Yard 1964–. Dir. Home Office Forensic Science Lab. Newcastle-upon-Tyne (1958-64).

WARDLAW, Henry (1378-1440). Scottish Divine who played a prominent part in founding St Andrews University (1411).

WATERS, Sir George A., born 1880 in Thurso, Caithness. Editor of the 'Scotsman' (1924-44).

WATERSTON, John James (1811-83) of Edinburgh. Physicist. Developed early Kinetic theory of gases.

WATSON, Benjamin P., born 1880 in Anstruther. Sometime Professor

Emeritus of Obstetrics and Gynaecology, Columbia Univ. New York.

WATSON, Sir Daril, born 1888 in Paisley? General, G.O.C. 2nd Div. (1940-41); Asst. Chief Imp. General Staff (1942); G.O.C.-in-C Western Commd. (1944-46); Quartermaster-General to the Forces (1946-47) etc.

WATSON, Sir James A.S., born 1889 in Dundee. Agricultural Attaché, Brit. Embassy, Washington (1942-44). Chief Scientific and Agricultural Adviser to Min. of Agric., and Director-General, Nat. Agric. Advisory Service (1948-54).

WATSON, James W., born 1915, educ. Edinburgh and Toronto. Prof. of Geography and Head of the Dept. of Geography, Edinburgh Univ., 1954–. Chief Geographer, Canada and Director of the Geographical Branch, Dept. of Mines and Tech. Surveys Canada (1949-54).

WATSON, Robert (1746-1838) of Elgin. Adventurer. Fought for American Independence. Sometime Napoleon's tutor in English, and President of Scots College, Paris.

WATSON, Robert, born 1894 in Aberdeenshire. Country representative for Ethiopia to the Food and Agricultural Organization of the United Nations, 1957–.

WATSON-WATT, Sir Robert Alexander, born 1892 in Brechin. Physicist. Appointed Scientific Adviser to the Air Ministry in 1940. Invented Radar.

WATT, Ian B., born 1916 in Perth. Deputy High Commissioner, Malta (1964). High Commissioner, Lesotho, 1966–.

WATT, James (1736-1819) of Greenock. Prolific inventor. Developed the improved steam engine; invented the condenser (1765), sun and planet gear (1784), the governor, water gauge, parallel motion, smokeless furnace and a letter copying machine.

WATT, W.M., born 1909 in Fife. Professor of Arabic and Islamic Studies. Visiting professor of Islamic Studies, Univ. of Toronto 1963–.

WAUGH, Sir Andrew Scott (1810-78) educ. Edinburgh. Major-General and Surveyor-General of India (1843).

WAUGH, Sir Arthur A., born 1891, educ. Edinburgh. Secretary, Dept. of Supply, Govt., of India (1943). Controller of Establishments, British Council (1948-54). Chairman, Salaries Commission, Ghana

(1956-57).

WAVERLEY, (John Anderson) 1st Viscount (1882-1958) of Eskbank. Administrator and Cabinet Minister. Home Sec. and Min. for Home Security (1939-40). The 'Anderson' Air Raid Shelter bears his name. Chancellor of the Exchequer in 1943.

WEBSTER, John H.D., born 1882 in Edinburgh. Radiologist. Sometime Emeritus Consultant, Middlesex Hosp. Published several works on Periodicity in Nature, Life, Mind and Diseases.

WEIR, James G., born 1887 in Dumfriesshire. Sometime Director of the Bank of England.

WEIR, Molly, of Glasgow. Character and Comedy actress, and writer. Became popular on radio as Tattie McIntosh in 'ITMA'; Aggie in 'Life with the Lyons' and Ivy McTweed in 'The McFlannels'.

WEIR, Robert H., born 1912 of Glasgow. Director-General, Gas Turbine Establishment, Pyestock, Farnborough 1960—.

WEMYSS, (Francis W.C. Douglas) Earl of (1818-1914) of Edinburgh. Politician and promoter of the volunteer system (1859 onwards) and the National Rifle Assoc.

WHYTT, Robert (1714-66) of Edinburgh. A pioneer Neurologist. One of the first to investigate reflex action.

WILKIE, Alexander M. (1917-66) of Glasgow. British Resident Commissioner, New Hebrides (1962-66).

WILKIE, Sir David (1785-1841) of Cults. Painter and etcher. In 1830 made painter extraordinary to the King. Elected R.A. in 1811.

WILSON, Alexander (1766-1813) of Paisley. Poet, Ornithologist and artist. Emigrated to the U.S. in 1794 and won wide recognition there. Published 'American Ornithology' (7 vols. 1808-14).

WILSON, Arthur G., born 1900 in Glasgow? Major-General. G.S.O. I. Australian Imperial Forces, U.K. and later Asst. Military Liaison Officer, Aust. High Commissioners Office U.K. till 1943. With Australian Forces in New Guinea, Philippines and Borneo (1943-45). Commanded the British Commonwealth Base, Japan (1946-47).

WILSON, Charles T.R. (1867-1959) of Glencourse. Pioneer in Atomic and Nuclear Physics. Prof. of Natural Philosophy at Cambridge (1925-34). Famous for his invention of the 'Wilson Cloud Chamber', an indispensible tool of modern physics ever since. Elected Fellow of the Royal Society.

WILSON, Sir Daniel (1816-92) of Edinburgh. Archaeologist. In 1853 became Professor of History and English Literature at Toronto.

WILSON, Isabel G.H., of Edinburgh? Sometime Principal Medical Officer, Ministry of Health (Retd.)

WILSON, James (1805-60) of Hawick. Economist. Became an authority on the Corn Laws and Currency. Founded the 'Economist'.

WILSON, James, born 1899 in Glasgow. Industrial Training Consultant. Sometime Director of Education and Training, British Motor Corp. Ltd.

WILSON, James S., born 1909 in Broughty Ferry. Air Vice-Marshal (Retd.), Lecturer, Institute of Hygiene, R.A.F. Halton 1965—.

WILSON, John (nicknamed 'Christopher North'), (1785-1858) of Paisley. Journalist and Poet. Elected to the Chair of Moral Philosophy in Edinburgh in 1820.

WILSON, John (1800-49) of Edinburgh. Singer. For years a favourite operatic tenor in London (Covent Garden and Drury Lane). Toured America and Canada.

WILSON, John (1804-75) of Lauder. Missionary in Bombay (1828-75). Sometime Vice-Chancellor of Bombay University.

WILSON, John Mackay (1804-34) of Tweedmouth. Writer and editor. Known for his 'Tales of the Borders' (6 vols.).

WILSON, Robert (1803-82) of Dunbar. Inventor of the screw propellor for ships, and a double-acting steam-hammer in 1861.

WILSON, Robert, Singer who popularised the old song 'Scotland the Brave', now regarded by many as the Scottish National Anthem.

WILSON, Samuel, born in America of Greenock parents. The original 'Uncle Sam' of America, and his wife was known as 'Aunt Betsy'. He was a meat packer, supplying the Colonial army in 1812.

WIMBERLEY, Douglas N., born 1896. Major-General Commanding the 51st Highland Div. (1941-43) in North Africa when Rommel was defeated at Alamein.

WISHART, George (c. 1513-46) of Kincardineshire. Reformer and Martyr. Translated the Swiss 'Confessions of Faith'. Was arrested at Cardinal Beaton's instance in 1546 and burned at St Andrews.

WITHERSPOON, Rev John (1722-94) from near Haddington. Theologian. Sometime Principal of Princeton, U.S.A. Was the only Cleric to sign the United States Declaration of Independence.

WOLFSON, Sir Isaac, born 1897 in Glasgow. Chain Stores Tycoon. Head of The Great Universal Stores Ltd.

WOOD, Alexander (1817-84). Advocated the use of the Hypodermic Syringe for injections in 1885.

WOODBURN, Arthur, born 1890 in Edinburgh. Parliamentary Sec., Ministry of Supply (1945-47); Sec. of State for Scotland (1947-50). Member, Select Committee on House of Commons Procedure (1956 - 68).

WRIGHT, Rev Ronald Selby, born 1908 in Edinburgh? Broadcaster known as the 'Radio Padre'. Toured all Commands during World War II. Chaplain for the Queen in Scotland 1963—.

Y

YOUNG, Alexander, born 1915 in Edinburgh. Director of Ordnance Services, Ministry of Defence, 1968—.

YOUNG, Andrew (1807-89) of Edinburgh. Schoolmaster, poet and Hymn writer. 'There is a Happy Land' his best known hymn.

YOUNG, Andrew John, born 1885 in Elgin. Clergyman and poet. Wrote many Nature poems incl: 'Boaz and Ruth' (1920); 'The White Blackbird' (1935); 'The Green Man' (1949); 'Into Hades' (1952). He also published Botanical essays. Was awarded the Queen's Medal for Poetry in 1952.

YOUNG, Arthur P., born 1885 in Ayrshire? Founder and Vice President, Institute of Works Managers. Chairman, Confederation of Management Assocs. (1938-48) and of Institute of Works Managers (1934-50).

YOUNG, James (1811-89) of Glasgow. Chemist and founder of the Mineral Oil Industry in Scotland. Discovered a method of distilling oil from shale. Was sometimes known as 'Paraffin Young'.

YOUNG, Ruth, of Dundee. Prof. of Surgery, Delhi Medical Coll. (1916-17); Director, Maternity and Child Welfare Bureau, Indian Red Cross (1931-35). Adviser Ethiopian Women's Work Assoc. on Welfare (1943) etc.

YOUNG, Thomas (1587-1655) of Perthshire. Puritan Divine. Was Milton's tutor till 1622 and later held charges at Hamburg and Essex.

YOUNG, Thomas, born 1893 of Kilmarnock? Major-General (1949); Director of Medical Services, Far East Land Forces (1948) and Director, Army Health (1949-53) (retired 53).

YOUNG, Sir William (1799-1887) of Falkirk. Sometime Chief Justice of Nova Scotia.

YOUNGER, John E.T., born 1888 in Dumfriesshire. Major-General. Asst. Director of Artillery, War Office (1938-39), Commander 3rd A.A. Div. (1940-42). General Staff Washington (1942-43).

YOUNGER, Sir William Ewan, born 1905 in Montrose. Chairman and Man. Director Scottish and Newcastle Breweries Ltd. 1960. Director Scottish Television, British Lininen Bank, etc.

YULE, Sir Henry (1820-89) of Inveresk. Geographer. Attained distinction with others in the restoration and development of the irrigation system of the Moguls.

INDEX

INVENTIONS and DISCOVERIES

MISSIONARIES

EXPLORERS

PRIME MINISTERS

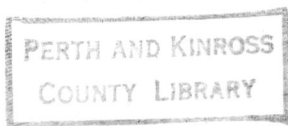